ALL THAT DUTCH

International Cultural Politics

001

00/00

All That Dutch
  Foreword   004
International Cultural Policy: Tradition of Innovation
  Jan Hoekema   006

Cultural Profile

A Strong Artistic Heartbeat
  Henk Pröpper   010
The Arts under a National Flag
  Valentijn Byvanck   014
There's Not Enough Craving – interview
  Charles Esche   019
Tulips and Windmills Forever
  Aaron Betsky   022
A Plea for More Cultural Institutes Abroad – interview
  Bert van Meggelen   026
Culture as Dynamic
  William Uricchio   029
Bring in the Cultivators – interview
  Jan Debbaut   034

Culture and Politics

Mutual Engagement
  Ben Hurkmans   038
A Curator is Not a Politician – interview
  Catherine David   042
On the Wrong Foot
  Dragan Klaic   047
Politics and Culture are Hard to Separate – interview
  Els van der Plas   053
Art as a Permanent Hint
  Jos de Putter   057
Throw Open the Shutters
  Boris Dittrich   060
Don't Jump on the Bandwagon – Start One Rolling Yourself – interview
  Chris Dercon   063

Culture and Economics

Living Apart Together
George Lawson   068
Culture and the Creative Economy
Rick van der Ploeg   070
Building Creative Capital
Joeri van den Steenhoven   076
Who is the Johan Cruyff of Dutch Rock 'n' Roll? – interview
Mir Wermuth   080
Close the Gap Between Art and Commerce
Femke Wolting   083
New Dutch Design: From the Inside Out
Peik Suyling   086
Thank God My Name Doesn't Sound Dutch – interviews
Sydney Neter, Barbara Truyen, Wouter Barendrecht   089

International Mediation

No Interior Without Exterior
Gitta Luiten   094
Visionary Netherlands
Ann Demeester and Maria Hlavajova   097
Reflection? What Reflection?
Bas Heijne   102
Important International Performances Twice a Month – interview
Johan Simons   105
Malaise – the Opportunity of a Lifetime
Thomas Michelon   108
Always a Free Port – interview
Alida Neslo   112

Culture for Real – interview
Masuhiro Sato   116

All That Dutch

Taco de Neef and Femke van Woerden-Tausk

The international cultural policy that the Netherlands has conducted over the past fifteen years is currently under discussion. The effectiveness of the ways in which our country presents itself to the outside world is no longer taken for granted. Within the framework of the Cultural Memorandum 2005 – 2008, this subject is now also on the political agenda. The crucial question is what we should do where, and why.

The Netherlands presents itself abroad as a motley collection of the international ambitions of artists and art institutions, with the government primarily playing a demand-oriented, supportive role. But is this sufficient? Shouldn't Dutch international cultural policy be more ambitious and focused on results, with clear objectives and the measured commitment of a limited number of methods of support? How broadly should these objectives be formulated? Do political, economic or social considerations carry any weight, or is culture the only thing that counts? The Fund for Amateur Art and the Performing Arts, the Foundation for the Production and Translation of Dutch Literature, the Mondriaan Foundation, and the initiator, the Service Centre for International Cultural Activities, hope this publication will act as a stimulus in sharpening public debate on Dutch international cultural politics.

"What should the Netherlands do where, and why?" We submitted this question to a number of art professionals, scholars and policymakers. Because international cultural exchange has political, social and economic significance in addition to the artistic, the discussion of international cultural policy cannot rest on artistic content alone. We asked our assembled writers to consider one of the four following themes: Culture and Politics, Culture and Economy, International Mediation, and Cultural Profile.

The Netherlands has no deliberately created cultural profile at the international level. Should we emphasize our 'Dutch identity' in the image that we project abroad? Is it perhaps worthwhile, especially in light of far-reaching globalization, to strive for a general profile of culture from the Netherlands? And what would be the components of a collective international promotion of such a 'Holland Image'?

The interests of culture and politics can be contradictory, because the cultural sector can at times have its own decidedly apolitical dynamics. How do these differing interests relate to one another? When are they complementary? Can culture be utilized to hasten the unification of Europe, or to improve contacts with Islamic countries?

The relationship between culture and the economy and the capitalization of creativity have received little attention in Dutch cultural policy until now – let alone that the international aspects of this relationship have been thought out. Which disciplines could profit from an active export policy? How should international cultural policy relate to economic policy? How can we further strengthen the international position of our creative industry?

It seems as though the Dutch cultural world is losing its connection with international developments. Have we become so involved with ourselves that we no longer pay any notice to what is happening around us? Why is international mediation important for keeping in touch with international developments and in what ways can this best take place?

'All That Dutch: International Cultural Politics' presents divergent perspectives – not cut-and-dried answers, but individual insights and opinions, some of them contemplative and more theoretical, others mainly practical and personal. They make it clear that although the Netherlands' participation in the international cultural arena is not unsuccessful, there are definitely improvements to be made. What clearly emerges is the necessity for a change of mentality: stimulating a more open, interested attitude within the Dutch cultural world and re-awakening its pioneering urge. An effective international policy fosters diversity, keeps things moving and leaves room for personal initiative. Clearer, more daring and explicit choices can be made within such a policy area and in the initiatives it supports.

On behalf of the editors, **Taco de Neef** (Mondriaan Foundation) and **Femke Van Woerden-Tausk** (SICA).

Taco de Neef and Femke van Woerden-Tausk

International Cultural Policy: Tradition of Innovation

"Amber feels like a cultural ambassador as she sells Dutch products to 'impeccably tailored businessmen' in her New York shop, which means she furnishes the gentleman in pinstriped suits with 'oliebollen', liquorice and Dutch shortcake cookies." – From a review by Clara Strijbosch of the book *De onfeilbare* by Clair Polders in the Volkskrant, April 8, 2005.

The above citation is an interesting example of the ineradicable stereotyping with which Dutch products – and not only windmills, tulips and cheese – are presented as promising items for cultural export. Granted, deep-fried dough balls, liquorice and shortcake cookies are forms of cultural heritage rarely seen in the literature on this subject.

International cultural policy, the topic of this extraordinary book, is about the export and import of cultural expression in virtually every possible discipline, and the images and profiles that we project of our country as well as our Dutch perceptions of other countries. Although Jan Debbaut may state in his contribution to this book that art is not 'cheese or tulip bulbs' – and strictly speaking he is quite right, of course – you cannot deny that such hardy perennials are part of Holland's image. When I recently gave a speech at the official opening of the Cheese Market in Alkmaar, the place was packed with foreigners, cameras at the ready, few of whom would afterwards have made their way to the nearby impressive new municipal Museum designed by Meccanoo.
So should we simply put a halt to our efforts to sell 'high culture' to the rest of the world? Certainly not. But we shouldn't be too bothered about the persistence of some of the well-worn components of the Dutch image; they're good for tourism – and The Netherlands Inc. puts the profits from mass tourism to good use. Artificial combinations of 'economic culture' and 'high culture' are not the answer, however. As Valentijn Byvanck correctly states in his essay, "There will always be friction between political and business interests on the one hand and cultural standing on the other." And that's not a bad thing, as long as we can keep these values well separated. No gigantic caravans behind royal visits, please, with trade delegations coming first and a few cultural vehicles bringing up the rear.
Rick van der Ploeg shows that 'culture and the creative economy' can be approached with much more subtlety. Financially, culture rates surprisingly highly, and is a booster for local, regional and national economies. When it comes to the role of culture in national and international policy, the contradistinction between 'instrumentalists' and 'autonomists' is outmoded, and without wanting to make too great of a leap, isn't the display, profiling and export of high quality art and culture itself a form of the public diplomacy currently so greatly in vogue?

'Original artistic highlights' (Byvanck) and established names both figure in international cultural policy. The unifying element is quality – a test which will always remain necessary, however difficult it may sometimes be to carry out. But it is still always easier than originality or inventiveness, which soon become empty words.

Thus Dutch international cultural policy is about the export and import of quality – and, I would add, diversity. And that's where it becomes interesting. Afterall, the Netherlands has for centuries been a freeport for other cultures that became integrated and started exporting in their turn. Around 10 years ago the slogan of State Secretary of Culture Aad Nuis was 'Freeport Holland'.

Since then we haven't found any generally accepted, snappy new paradigm. Nor are the times in our favour. Our worldview has narrowed since 2001 – not surprisingly, but disquieting indeed. Now that the easy but politically correct integration mantras no longer seem to work, the identity of the Netherlands is adrift and we have to face the fact and learn how to live with a deeply changed, coloured Netherlands. We're struggling with this in the cultural sector too. Moroccan writers like Kader Abdolah, Abdelkader Benali, and quite a few others are practically cuddled to death; Morocco and Turkey as countries of origin are seen as priorities in international cultural policy, and diversity is avowed. Away with the boring white uniformity ensconced within the concentric rings of canals in the city centres. But it's less clear what should take its place.

Against this confusing background – or even 'malaise as the opportunity of a lifetime' as Thomas Michelon puts it – we must seek our way in international cultural policy. But I do not believe we need to forge a completely new path. We must above all be proud of what we have accomplished and of what lies at the foundation of our international cultural policy. In his essay in this book, Aaron Betsky points the way to a new self-confidence. We may not yet be ready to present a fully-formed new identity, and we may be afraid of foreigners, Europe and Polish plumbers, but beyond its borders the Netherlands is performing well. That's my opinion, and that of most of the authors of this book, with the exception of Debbaut who left the country.

I believe we have good reason for pride. The system of cultural subsidies for international presentation and profiling that has been in place since the mid-nineties is certainly well organised, and is the cause of jealousy in many countries, from Slovenia to the other founding members of the EU. Admittedly, we have no British Councils, Goethe Institutes, Cervantes Houses or Maisons Descartes, but we do have a well-functioning system of large subsidies administered jointly by the Ministry of Foreign Affairs and the Ministry of Education, Cultural Affairs and Science (the famous – or infamous – Hgis-C) and smaller subsidies administered by the two Ministries separately. Altogether, the government and other organisations and foundations invest twenty to thirty million euros on international promotion, which is not to be sneezed at.

Since we don't incur the considerable costs that come with bricks–and–mortar, we can achieve great value-for-money by targeting subsidies at intensifying and profiling cultural activities abroad as well as the import of high-quality foreign culture (albeit to a lesser extent). But the race is not won. A classic example is the Hgis-C's hesitation in awarding a subsidy to Dutch fashion designers Viktor and Rolf for an exhibition at the Fashion Museum of the Louvre, the argument being that "those boys already earn enough money as it is." Fortunately, after further discussion, the subsidy was awarded. The Netherlands is a leader across a broad range of disciplines, from design and fashion to architecture and modern music. Other sectors, such as the visual arts, do less well in the eyes of many observers, but there's no lack of big names here either. The first artwork I came upon in Johannesburg's magnificent Supreme Court was by Marlene Dumas. Proud? Yes, I'm proud, and I even feel a tinge of Orange glow. Why not? I have the same feeling when I see the Netherlands Dance Theater or go to the Concertgebouw, even though a very small minority of the performers are Dutch.

This fascinating book presents a broad range of opinion and recommendations concerning international cultural policy. The guiding principle, it would seem, is to 'open wide to the rest of the world' (Boris Dittrich), with in joint second place the 'will to experiment' (Charles Esche) and the promotion of 'original artistic highlights'. I'm particularly curious about what the new marketing slogan will be, for Charles Esche's facile opinion that a museum's mandate could be changed from attracting the public to 'increasing the creative power in your area' would seem to be at odds with some of the fundamental principles of this Cabinet and more particularly, of the State Secretary of Culture. Luckily, Eindhoven is a healthy and economically promising region. This book confronts us once again with the intriguing question of how people look at us, and warns us against complacency; there is certainly no reason for the latter. The international aspect of art and culture is under pressure, and the current discussion on cultural policy tends to be national or regional in character. There is nothing wrong with that, as long as we remain aware that many fascinating things go on beyond our borders and that cultural exchange between other countries and the Netherlands can have a positive effect. Throughout the centuries, our country has had much to offer to the world, but also much to gain: 'Freeport Holland'. That almost seems like an old-fashioned concept after all that has recently happened in our own and other societies, but it is not. If this book can contribute to the forming of opinion on an hospitable, modern, creative and innovative Netherlands, fine. If it's a critical mirror, that's fine too. And if 'Freeport' sounds a bit hackneyed, then sometime soon we'll have to hold a competition for a new paradigm. I'm already sending the jury my provisional entry: tradition of innovation.

Jan Hoekema is director of the Cultural, Education and Research Division of the Ministry of Foreign Affairs and the Dutch ambassador for International Co-operation. From 1994 to 2002 he was a member of the parliamentary party D66.

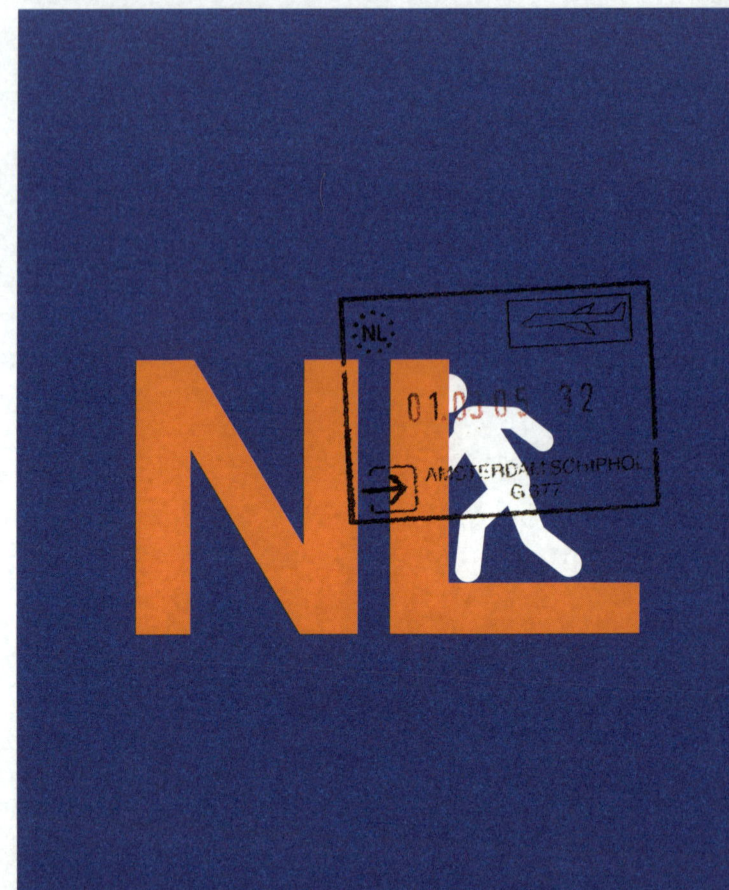

I came to the Netherlands on 1st of March.
I was really looking forward to living in the Netherlands.

Cultural
Profile

A Strong Artistic Heartbeat

In her book, *Illness as Metaphor*, Susan Sontag magisterially teases out our tendency to view countries in terms of sickness and health. In the public imagination there are healthy countries and there are sick countries. This is of course not a static phenomenon: a healthy country can become sick. Until quite recently Holland was seen as the reservoir or breeding ground of so-called 'Hollanditis'. According to some, this was an ailment arising out of moral weakness and an inadequate vision of broader world politics; to others, it was actually a fortunate condition bringing with it healthy insights and contributing to East-West détente. There seem to be various ways of diagnosing illness and they raise a number of questions: should medicines be prescribed (soothing words, kill-or-cure remedies); is the illness catching and should it therefore be controlled at all costs; or is it actually a sign of good health – a form of self-purification?

In its time, 'Hollanditis' was seen by transatlantic hawks as an exceptionally dangerous, extremely infectious disease. It was eroding the backbone of the West and in the Netherlands the ailment affected all sorts of fields beside that of geopolitical analysis. Holland's policy of tolerance and moral freedom already contained the germs of the moral weakness identified today.

The way in which these images of sickness and health are constructed also reveals a tendency to allow this sort of 'analysis' to become totalitarian: it describes the whole, and any undesirable qualities attributed to a country are seen as a result of the appalling condition already diagnosed.

The words 'sick' and 'weak' (decadent) are used in contrast to 'healthy' and 'strong' (vital). In a given period, Germany may be called 'the sick old man of Europe', but there is no reason this fate should not strike France. At the moment the whole of Europe is associated with old age and ill-health.

In the 1990s, Holland was in the peak of health and it wasn't only Holland that thought so ('we're doing great'); the outside world too was impressed by its youth, vitality and omnipresence. Never before had the German, French and American press been so positive about the Netherlands, and it seemed people were starting to wonder whether the peculiar weakness of character behind the tolerance policy might have its hidden strengths. The exceptionally advantageous economic climate turned out to be linked, even in the context of the Dutch 'image', in a relatively one-dimensional but extremely clear way to the idea of the '*polder* model': where there's a will there's a way. This recipe was seen as a panacea all over the world, an alchemist's potion that could turn our history, our geographical location, our battles with the sea into coin of the realm: from mud to gold. Classical images lay at the root of the very words 'polder model', and these were coupled with contemporary ideas of dialogue and exchange. History, present and future appeared to join in happy confluence. The sun never set on the Netherlands. It is no coincidence that during this period, people became interested in what we call 'public diplomacy'. After all, Holland had some important messages to bring to the world, and had we not always had a rather messianic outlook? Who, we thought, would *not* want to receive a healthy and healing Messiah – health is infectious too.

It was in this light that the idea of experimental Holland was born: Holland, the social laboratory, associated with the unprecedentedly innovative powers that characterized Dutch art and especially architecture, fashion, photography and design. It was as if Holland was organized according to a single all-embracing concept in which legislation, the cultivation of public opinion and artistic creation all went hand in hand and were moreover visible and accessible to all citizens – a super-democracy. For the first time, Holland came close to realizing the concept of 'branding' – promoting a unique cultural profile.

How healthy can you get?

Then Holland was again struck down by illness or, more accurately, the symptoms surfaced of a disease which, after a long, strangely unnoticed period of incubation, proved extremely dangerous. And the reaction to this new situation has now reached a pitch of hysteria. Public opinion, so highly valued, turned out to be a stinking morass of dissenting views. Unity and democratic consciousness were hard to find; the polder model was finished. This Dutch illness was new in the sense that suddenly everyone was diagnosing it, both at home and abroad, and (certainly in Holland) the crudest quack doctors had the loudest voices, raging in their fever rather than addressing its cause.

As always, we respond by demanding, in our panic, that the arts immediately adopt a more socially-minded approach and provide social commentary. Where else can we look for rescue? Where else might we find a cure?

This is the climate in which the present discussion of Holland's cultural image and international significance is taking place. Actually, the timing is perfect. Although I am reluctant to accept the rhythm of birth, life and decay, sickness and health as the underlying beat of life – such metaphors are too crude for most purposes – it seems from the contributions to this chapter that most of the authors regard present times and present policies as little short of depressing. Only Aron Betsky (the Director of the NAi) starts out from the classical idea of culture as malleable and sees in the Netherlands a powerful combination of patronage and artistic achievement. He emphasizes the fact that artificiality is virtually a fundamental principle of our landscape and society, and he sees great vitality in it, first and foremost in architecture and design. With the exception of Bert van Meggelen, (Director of Stichting Maatwerk) all the contributors to this chapter are specialists in the field of fine arts. In my opinion they give an unnecessarily negative cast to the Dutch 'image'. From a purely artistic point of view, I think much important work is being done here, in a wide range of disciplines. It is surely indisputable that over the last fifteen years the international presence of Dutch art and artists has increased tremendously. Taking the intrinsic value and autonomy of the artwork as a major starting point, a more general (Dutch) profile has come to be seen as unimportant or even undesirable. I would support the view that some of the arts, partly as a result of this, may have perhaps become too divorced from reality – even legitimately so – and that there is room for a greater degree of realism in artistic creation. But this should be less about gossip and the word on the street than about a world that sets us thinking about our own.

Most of the contributions in this chapter mention the threat of provincialism that haunts the Netherlands. We may be very internationally oriented, but only where the export of art is concerned. 'Much export, little import, and little participation in international discourse', is how we might summarize this chapter. Jan Debbaut (Head of Collections at the Tate Gallery in London) is of the opinion that a great deal of good art is created in Holland, but that Holland does not exist internationally: we have no image abroad. Dutch critics do not play any meaningful role outside their own country, he says; there is too little participation in international networks; Holland has little influence on international public opinion. Amongst others, Charles Esche (Director of the Van Abbe Museum), links this to the fact that within Holland far too little use is made of the presence of foreigners. If invited at all, they are merely tolerated and given little or no room to make their mark. The Dutch cultural profile could profit from being more hospitable and taking more of an interest in foreigners' opinions about our culture and its development.

Esche also detects a certain moroseness, a culture of self-castigation and excessive introspection, without any hope of achieving a more balanced self-image. There is too little opportunity for experimentation. This idea ties in neatly with Director of the Zeeuws Museum Valentijn Byvanck's insight that when thinking of a Dutch cultural profile, we should give priority to the export of our most original and outstanding products. Although he feels we should not confuse art with identity, a sensitive fictional combination of different but related images might help us to present Dutch culture. Byvanck would have no objection to the creation of new clichés in an attempt to foster the anomalous, the progressive and the innovative.

Bert van Meggelen clearly favours institutions and symbols, meaning a major physical and spiritual presence abroad and the export of images that tell stories about our country. He mentions Ben van Berkel's Rotterdam Bridge (The Swan) as a possible symbol. Everyone agrees, however, that art should not be used as a way of 'making things better'.

As I tried to make clear in my introductory paragraphs, images and stories about our country arise as if spontaneously. They are more or less coherent fictions, whether created intentionally or not. Although the Dutch themselves refuse to believe it, for a small country Holland has quite a strong international profile. Few countries are associated with so much health and so much sickness. In the contributions to this book, however, our cultural profile is seen as under-developed. I regard striving towards a healthy cultural image without investing in the actual internationalisation of our culture as a disastrous path.

We must not overestimate the extent to which we can create images of ourselves; in reality, people stick labels on us. We can influence the way we are seen, however, and this requires greater openness to other countries, rather than a frenetic search for identity. If the notion that we have the power to shape our own society is a neatly tailored fiction that prompts perpetual innovation and openness to the opinions and insights of foreigners, then there is little to be said against this particular myth of the 1990s. The authors in this chapter favour a sensitive handling of images, however. Powerful artistry is essential. We can then look for ways of creating our own profile by, for example, adopting an artistic approach to public events, staging state-sponsored happenings with a strong artistic heartbeat. All the same, there is no alternative to investing much more in participation on an international level, developing the appropriate networks and helping to shape public opinion.

Henk Pröpper is director of the Foundation for the Production and Translation of Dutch Literature. From 1998 to 2003, he was director of the Institut Néerlandais in Paris. He has published a novel and a collection of essays and writes for newspapers and periodicals.

The Arts Under a National Flag
Cultural Policy and National Identity

For an accurate analysis of Dutch international cultural policy, clear definitions are essential. 'International cultural policy' is a misleading term for an untidy collection of policy programmes devoted to government-supported promotion of the arts abroad. The term 'culture' is too broad for these programmes, as Dutch culture includes everything that takes place within the borders of this country. The term 'international' implies that there are discussions with other countries about the fundamentals and the form of the policy, while it is in fact a policy for the promotion of arts and art products that is entirely shaped by Dutch government officials.

This promotion always takes place within an identity framework. Artistic activities presented under a national flag automatically raise the question of what the work and the flag have to do with each other. That goes for all Dutch exports: cheese, hydraulic engineering, even tolerance. But in the case of the arts the link goes deeper. This may be the result of age-old discourses about national character, illustrated by examples from 17th-century paintings. We do in any case consider works of art more eloquent than other products. We believe that the arts say something essential about us and our national identity.

I suspect that this entanglement of art and identity has produced the misleading term 'cultural policy'. We feel that when we export art we are also exporting something greater: a piece of our culture. Yet the idea that policy should therefore be actively involved in shaping an identity is a misconception. The arts can often better be exported as a collection of highlights from which historians can distil an identity later on.

The term 'identity' dominates thinking about present-day Holland. The country is taking its first uncertain steps towards becoming a multicultural society. Forced contact with population groups that have different views on life, different tastes and religions is leading to constant conflict, and the opposing parties invariably seek justification in the discourse on identity. This discourse pervades all sections of society, sometimes exemplified by the magnification of differences between an imaginary 'us' and 'them', at other times by calls for a historical canon that can link the 'native' Dutch and the immigrant populations to a common past.

This call for a canon is one of the recurring rituals of nation-building, which always involves the use of fictions that are carefully distilled from a vast number of narratives and customs. These fictions, accurately described by historian Eric Hobsbawm as 'invented traditions', are hammered out and refined over the years by all sorts of social groups in a battle of opposing interests. The result is a national image that is no longer questioned. In this connection, historian Hugh Trevor-Roper describes the way Scots, kilts and bagpipes became inseparably linked. The more firmly national identity was asserted, the less accidental the historical linkage between these attributes appeared to be. Along with the relevant national holidays and flag displays, kilts and bagpipes became symbols of a national community. Such community narratives are among the most convincing fictions of the modern world.[1]

The fictions of our lowland country are easy to name. The Dutch are down-to-earth, hard-working, business-minded, tolerant, straightforward and averse to frivolity. The exported symbols of these national characteristics – clogs (down-to-earth), flowers (super-farmers) and permissive policies (tolerance) – are recognised everywhere as part of Dutch heritage.

Whereas these fictions were originally intended to define and unite our own group, they are now almost entirely aimed at influencing the outside world. This process has even been given a special name: 'branding', a form of national self-promotion in which a country is launched onto the market as if it were a product. Such identity advertising makes Holland suitable for export with the help of several attractive images that confirm international expectations.

The purpose of branding is to foster goodwill. A small photographic exhibition accompanying a diplomatic visit or an artistic performance at the start of an international conference is the high-brow equivalent of the 'Holland House' that graces every major international event with its raw herring, cheese and girls in Zeeland costumes, or the ubiquitous use of Delft Blue or Vermeer reproductions on Dutch export packaging. Politicians blaze these images abroad. Businessmen trade in them. The aim in both cases is instant recognition and approval. The controversial statement by former Dutch Cabinet minister Elco Brinkman that culture is a lubricant for politics has lost none of its force. Fostering goodwill that can be turned to Holland's advantage in other areas may be as good a reason as any to export Dutch art. In international politics, art is the continuation of diplomacy by other means.

However, this view of the arts is diametrically opposed to the image propagated within the arts world itself. The view encouraged by business and political interests is that the arts unite people, bringing them closer together, overcoming differences and promoting well-being. This normative view emphasises a static, traditional and uniform image of the arts. The view within the arts world, on the other hand, is that art is ever-changing, innovative and multiform. This suggests that, even if the arts can bring people together and overcome differences, they may also divide people and sharpen contradictions. They can give comfort and pleasure, but they can also be painful, disconcerting and offensive. Such pluriform images are obviously at odds with the idea of a uniform national culture.

Dealing creatively with the conflict between these two views of art is a prerequisite for an effective arts policy, and necessitates a two-track strategy. On the one hand, there should be no hesitation to use Dutch clichés when promoting new cultural works. The outside world readily understands things that fit in with images built up over the centuries. Rather than ignore or suppress them, effective policy should use them with flexibility and subtlety. At the same time, officials, policymakers and funding agencies need to cherish unconventional art and treat it as an equally worthy member of the Dutch cultural family. It is above all this kind of art that enriches the image of Dutch culture abroad and so helps promote a less one-sided picture of Dutch identity.

Not surprisingly, the most successful Dutch arts policies have been founded on old reputations. Since the 17th century the Netherlands has had a formidable reputation in the field of painting. Thousands of people all over the world study the paintings of the Golden Age which, according to conventional wisdom, displayed a unique sense of realism in their focus on the everyday and their avoidance of grand gestures and aesthetic exaggeration. Over the centuries the same reputation has extended to almost all Dutch painters. Van Gogh is praised for his focus on the everyday and Mondrian for his down-to-earth rationality. The ingredients of this reputation can also be clearly seen in other disciplines. Dutch architecture and design are renowned for being functional, free, aware of their own artificiality but devoid of frills, neo-modern. Dutch cinema and photography follow the same pattern, each emphasising the documentary genre, which is dominated by the same focus on everyday reality and economical use of the imagination.

All this is very much in keeping with our national fictions. Nothing sells better abroad than Dutch painting, architectural modernism (or hyper-modernism) and functional design. It would be a diplomatic and sensory blunder of the first order not to give these manifestations of our culture a privileged position in our international arts policy.

The second strategy is more difficult. Endless repetition of the same national fictions has left the world unreceptive to alternatives. Foreigners find it hard to imagine that the Dutch are sometimes better at music than at visual arts, that they produce dance theatre and fashion as well as photography and that they can write literature as well as invoices. The outside world's bewilderment at recent signs of Dutch intolerance is clear evidence that national fictions die hard, even despite countless indications to the contrary.

Some of these 'different' works of art can conceivably be fitted in at the margins of convention. The Amsterdam School in the field of architecture, Carel Willink in the visual arts, Orkater in theatre, Victor and Rolf in fashion and the VJ and computer/video artist Geert Mul can easily be presented as exceptions that prove the Dutch rule.

The real question, however, is what to do with Dutch art that does not fit into stereotyped branding – art that clashes with the political notion of culture as a unifying element and cannot be combined with business or political interests. Though renowned in the international art world, the paintings of Kiki Lamers, who is about to appear before a French court on pornography charges, are unlikely to be found on display in a Holland House. Nor will there be any hurry to translate the collected works of Theo van Gogh and hand out copies at international summits. Such works are simply not suited for lubricating international relations. But should they therefore be ignored?

These artists and their works are an important part of Dutch cultural heritage. Moreover, they often greatly enhance the domestic image of culture, for their reputation has been built up within the disciplines of visual art, theatre, cinema and so on, independent of business or political interests. If Holland is to gain prestige from their works, this will, for the time being, be chiefly within the art world itself. In the long run, however, it is these works that will enjoy the greatest reputation. They do not combine well with other areas of life, but they sow the seeds for a new cultural standing which in time will influence Dutch identity.

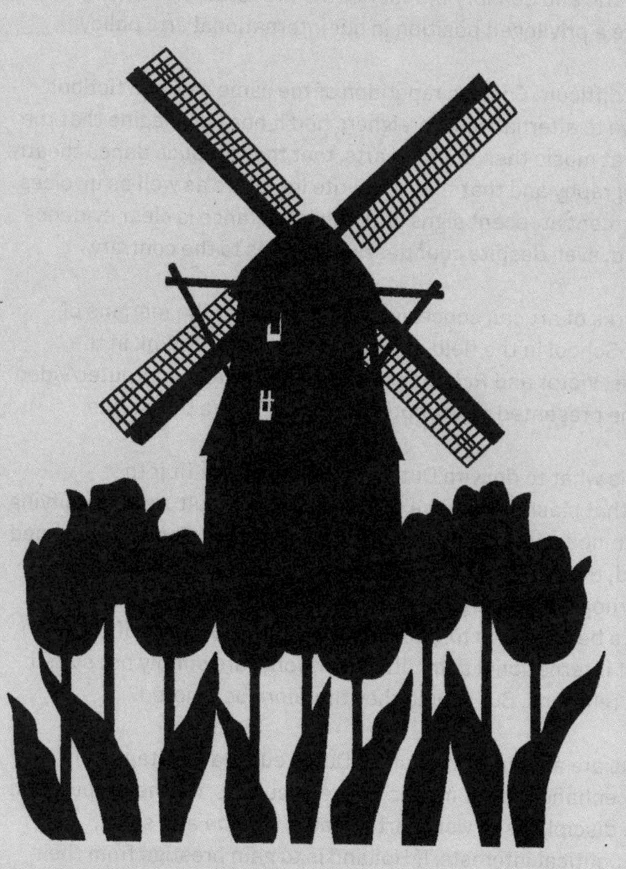

though I forgot about it,
realised that windmills and tulips are still the symbols of Dutch.

in keeping with our national fictions. Nothing sells better abroad
 architectural modernism (or hyper-modernism) and functional
 diplomatic and sensory blunder of the first order not to give these
ir culture a privileged position in our international arts policy.

is more difficult. Endless repetition of the same national fictions
receptive to alternatives. Foreigners find it hard to imagine that the
s better at music than at visual arts, that they produce dance theatre
is photography and that they can write literature as well as invoices.
bewilderment at recent signs of Dutch intolerance is clear evidence
s die hard, even despite countless indications to the contrary.

rent' works of art can conceivably be fitted in at the margins of
sterdam School in the field of architecture, Carel Willink in the
n theatre, Victor and Rolf in fashion and the VJ and computer/video
easily be presented as exceptions that prove the Dutch rule.

owever, is what to do with Dutch art that does not fit into
g – art that clashes with the political notion of culture as a unifying
be combined with business or political interests. Though renowned
art world, the paintings of Kiki Lamers, who is about to appear
t on pornography charges, are unlikely to be found on display in a
will there be any hurry to translate the collected works of Theo van
opies at international summits. Such works are simply not suited
national relations. But should they therefore be ignored?

eir works are an important part of Dutch cultural heritage.
 greatly enhance the domestic image of culture, for their reputation
thin the disciplines of visual art, theatre, cinema and so on,
ness or political interests. If Holland is to gain prestige from their
he time being, be chiefly within the art world itself. In the long run,
works that will enjoy the greatest reputation. They do not combine
s of life, but they sow the seeds for a new cultural standing which in
utch identity.

investment from the shrewd businessman and super-promoter Char
work changed the stiff, soporific reputation of British art for decade:
a sudden British artists were hot. Sexy artzines and East End galleri
mushrooms. Everyone realised that the British had something to say
Around the same time the Dogma group was launched by such Danis
von Trier and Thomas Vinterberg. Their new 'direct cinema', which set
reality that was not embellished or dramatised by special effects, fo
the world on Denmark.

One could argue about whether these examples are really permanen
that will be used to say something about Dutch, British or Danish ide
books about the twentieth century – but we simply cannot tell yet, fo
not yet become a tradition. Despite what we keep on telling ourselve
between works of art and their country of origin is not so much natu
as plausible, important, interesting or advantageous to a particular
generations will decide whether these new reputations have come t
words, whether they have become a self-evident part of the nationa

The role of the government in creating, or indeed disseminating, the:
fictions is a very limited one. While Dutch diplomats may wax enthus
skills of Dutch footballers, I can hardly imagine British or Danish fore
rushing to identify their countries with Tracy Emin's soiled bed or the
incest film The Celebration (Festen). Yet not only have both works gr
their countries' reputations, they have also enabled them to qualify
national images.

This is where the government can act as a catalyst. It can draw othe
attention to art that has not achieved the same success as the Britp
never will. However, it must do so outside the framework of national
achieve this, it needs to accept a non-normative, dynamic definition
also have to map out a promotional route which, independent of poli
interests, relies on evaluations by the art world itself. There are plen
that can perform this task, and their assessments should serve as a
of art that is too odd, loud, uncongenial or abstract to give foreign vis
conferences or embassy parties the required lustre.

The Dutch creators.
I already knew and I became to know more.

The best instances of this sort of work develop into counter-fictions. If we want to find such an example in Holland, we need to step outside the world of the arts and into the world of Dutch football, known for decades for its dazzling beauty, imagination and technical sophistication: the Dutch as the Brazilians of Europe! Foreigners' appreciation of characteristics which both here and abroad are regarded as un-Dutch has caused something of a national 'conversion'. The Dutch would rather see their teams lose elegantly than win at any price. No-frills efficiency and thoroughness are not the things that get the hearts of Dutch football fans racing.

There are similar examples to be found in the European art world. In the 1990s, the British visual arts world was jolted awake by the soothingly named Britpack art of Damien Hirst, Tracy Emin and Sam Taylor-Wood. In one fell swoop, spurred on by investment from the shrewd businessman and super-promoter Charles Saatchi, their work changed the stiff, soporific reputation of British art for decades to come. All of a sudden British artists were hot. Sexy artzines and East End galleries sprang up like mushrooms. Everyone realised that the British had something to say in the visual arts. Around the same time the Dogma group was launched by such Danish directors as Lars von Trier and Thomas Vinterberg. Their new 'direct cinema', which set out to portray raw reality that was not embellished or dramatised by special effects, focused the eyes of the world on Denmark.

One could argue about whether these examples are really permanent counter-fictions that will be used to say something about Dutch, British or Danish identity in future books about the twentieth century – but we simply cannot tell yet, for the invention has not yet become a tradition. Despite what we keep on telling ourselves, the relationship between works of art and their country of origin is not so much natural or authentic as plausible, important, interesting or advantageous to a particular group. Future generations will decide whether these new reputations have come to stay – in other words, whether they have become a self-evident part of the national image.

The role of the government in creating, or indeed disseminating, these cultural counter-fictions is a very limited one. While Dutch diplomats may wax enthusiastic about the skills of Dutch footballers, I can hardly imagine British or Danish foreign attachés rushing to identify their countries with Tracy Emin's soiled bed or the equally famous incest film The Celebration (Festen). Yet not only have both works greatly enhanced their countries' reputations, they have also enabled them to qualify conventional national images.

This is where the government can act as a catalyst. It can draw other countries' attention to art that has not achieved the same success as the Britpack and perhaps never will. However, it must do so outside the framework of national identity. If it is to achieve this, it needs to accept a non-normative, dynamic definition of the arts. It will also have to map out a promotional route which, independent of political and business interests, relies on evaluations by the art world itself. There are plenty of organisations that can perform this task, and their assessments should serve as a guide to the export of art that is too odd, loud, uncongenial or abstract to give foreign visits, international conferences or embassy parties the required lustre.

International competitions should be the primary venue for such dissemination of works of art. The earliest example of this type of platform was the world exhibition, a traditional showcase for national grandeur. It has, of course, long since been overtaken in prominence by successors such as the Olympic Games, the Eurovision Song Contest, the World Cup and the Venice and São Paulo Biennales. The great thing about such events is that countries can submit artistic highlights without having to present instantly recognisable or stereotyped images of themselves. In fact, they can even do the opposite. Some years ago, Germany sent a band consisting of Turkish immigrants to the Eurovision Song Contest. Curator Rein Wolfs selected three foreign artists who live in Holland for the Dutch pavilion at the Venice Biennale. Under the ironic title We are the World, he presented Carlos Amorales, Alicia Framis and Meshac Gaba along with two artists born and bred in Holland to represent the Dutch art world.

It is not hard to make statements about identity in the context of Rein Wolfs' entry. It could be argued that sending foreign artists to Venice represents a new pluriform perception of national identity. Alternatively, it could be argued that this is in keeping with the Dutch tradition of embracing cultural differences without exposing or feeling the pain involved in truly accepting those differences. Either interpretation may influence ideas about Dutch art and Holland itself. However, such statements about identity should not play any part in the selection of the biennial curator by the Mondriaan Foundation, or in the curator's selection of specific artists.

There will always be friction between political and business interests on the one hand and cultural standing on the other. There are plenty of examples of how the arts can successfully be used in international political negotiations. Yet the fact remains that if art is to unite people it must be mild and inoffensive, which means it is not free to develop in its own way. The choice will therefore continue to be based on existing preconceptions that the Dutch do not produce surrealistic art, have no musical tradition worth mentioning and have never heard of postmodernism. An arts policy geared to the export of original artistic highlights would challenge these preconceptions and help to shape national identity without explicitly setting out to do so.

Valentijn Byvanck is the director of the Zeeuws Museum in Middelburg. From 1999 to 2002 he worked for Witte de With, centre for contemporary art in Rotterdam. His most recent publication is *Superstudio: The Middelburg Lectures* (2005).

1 - Eric Hobsbawm and Terence Ranger, *The Invention of Tradition* (Cambridge: Cambridge University Press, 1983, Canto, 2004); Hugh Trevor-Roper, "The Invention of Tradition: The Highland Tradition of Scotland", in Hobsbawm and Ranger, *Invention of Tradition*, pp.15-42. See olso: Benedict Anderson, *Imagined Communities: Reflections on the Origin and Spread of Nationalism* (London and New York: Verso 1983, revised edition 1991).

There's Not Enough Craving

Charles Esche interviewed by *Sacha Bronwasser*

Charles Esche hopes to remain Director of the Van Abbemuseum in Eindhoven for ten years. He needs that much time to transform the museum into what he calls 'a power plant'. If he succeeds, the museum will function in a completely different way, benefiting the region and perhaps the entire country - though for Esche, that is decidedly a side effect. Benefit to the nation must never be a deciding factor in the policy of museums and other institutions. "People want to restore the experimental status of the Netherlands without the accompanying social woes. That's absurd and impossible." Charles Esche questions the whole idea of cultural profiling, and football proves to be a useful analogy.

"You can think up all sorts of tactics to improve the Netherlands' image abroad. But does anyone ever pause to consider just why they would want to? It can't be to get more people to visit the Netherlands. Is it really necessary? What do they want to achieve?"

Esche taught at the Rijksakademie before becoming the museum director in Eindhoven. "When I first came to the Netherlands my cultural profile of the country was that it had once been an interesting place, but now no longer was. I had a fairly clichéd idea of a Calvinist trading nation that was very individualistic and therefore very tolerant; this represented the Netherlands for me until 1979, 1980. Then came Reagan and Thatcher, and the whole social democratic ethos was dismantled. Mainland Europe, including the Netherlands, did not react. The Netherlands went into decline."

"What remained was weighted towards the individual, noticeable in Dutch art as well as in football. The Dutch are so highly individualistic that they can't work together. For twenty years now with the best football players in the world they can't win the World Cup.

"It's also the reason they can't confer. Coming from England, I was accustomed to the conference practice of passing statements from one person to the next as in a relay race. The idea that ultimately emerges is very far removed from the starting point. Here everyone states their position, then at the end the most senior manager lays all their statements side by side on the table and makes a decision. Individualism that preserves hierarchy - strange, isn't it?

"In art, this results in little or no collaboration. If you were to bring artists together, like the Young British Artists in the nineties in England, it wouldn't last long. People want to prove their individuality, and that stands in the way of the collective.

"A good example of what does not work is the Rijkakademie - a great institution to which I am devoted. The conditions there are excellent, the facilities splendid, and the international network is unsurpassed. I would recommend it to every artist. And yet many foreign students feel completely isolated there, because the Dutch students hardly mix at all with the foreigners. On top of that, they are located in a city (Amsterdam) that is a cultural backwater. It's the city you're in, along with the circles in which you move, that influences much of your work during your art student period. So the foreigners seek each other out. For some time now, the most interesting art in the Netherlands has been made by people who are not ethnically Dutch. Yael Bartana and Otto Berchem are good examples.

"Individualism, by the way, need not be negative. It leads directly to that famous Dutch tolerance: I can do what I want; you can do what you want. The basic idea is that you must remain yourself. That idea is very deeply rooted. It also explains why it's almost impossible to speak of 'Dutch art'.

"What has been lost is the notion of the experiment, the sense of order combined with playfulness, which existed here until the eighties. There were inventors and risk-takers in Dutch art and design back then. They're still around, but as individuals, not specifically Dutch. Take Rem Koolhaas: he is world famous, but not considered Dutch in the way that De Stijl was. Another case, in my own field, is that of Jean Leering (Director of the Van Abbemuseum, 1961-1973), the great experimenter. He remains underrated and totally ignored.

"In the eighties there was a shift toward conservatism - not necessarily to the right, more a marking of time. I don't know if experimentation was lost then, or if it went underground; but then I've never been able to locate an underground in the Netherlands. What I do see is a tendency towards conservatism.

"No institutions have emerged in the Netherlands in the past fifteen years that are seriously concerned with art. The last initiative was Witte de With in 1990 in Rotterdam. De Appel, the Stedelijk, Montevideo... they do their best, but where's the vitality? Where's the innovation? In the institutional sphere there's no development whatsoever. There is, however, one interesting organisation that arose without a governmental plan or subsidy, the SMART Project Space; but one institution is not enough, and its future is insecure. What are we going to do? Give them the money that the 'old' institutions no longer receive? Part of the problem is the subsidy system, which tends to obstruct development. If you want a creative country, you need vitality, conflict, turbulence. But the whole system smothers vitality and tension.

"You can't blame the institutions. Pointing a finger at the Stedelijk Museum is totally absurd. Do you think that in London they look to the Tate for answers? You have to turn things around. Why did Tate Modern come into being? Because in the 1990s there was a tremendous amount of interest in contemporary art. Without the YBAs, Tate Modern would never have been built. You don't build an institution in a vacuum. You need the energy and vitality of a community that is interested and supportive. That's what counts, irrespective of what the Stedelijk does. Let the Stedelijk be, it's irrelevant. The responsibility lies with us, as individuals. If the system doesn't work the way you want it to, do it yourself!

"There's not enough craving, that compulsive inner need that something *has to* happen. I come from the punk generation. 'Do-it-yourself' was the attitude and the answer, and I miss that. So do the artists who come from other countries where they *do* have to fend for themselves. They find the expectant attitude here cumbersome, hobbling, and tiring.

"I see too much analysis and too much self-castigation in the Netherlands, which wasn't the case before. People want to map out the entire situation (this publication is an example) and then draw up a plan. We should forget about that, and say: *Okay*, we're in a bad way, what'll we do? And just follow our noses and concentrate on what we're doing, taking the risk that it will fail. It's only art. We should always remember that while art is extremely important it is also exceedingly unimportant. Football, on the other hand, is never unimportant!

"Take subsidies for example. How can we redistribute this money in a dynamic way? How can we support truly new activities? Perhaps we should give start-up money a lot of new initiatives, and then continue to support the two or three that thrill.

"Another example is the creation of work spaces. Innovative art usually arises in places where people can occupy a cheap space together. When high rents push artists' studios out of the city centre to properly organized, ready-made spaces elsewhere, they lose much of their character.

"Trying to bring back the experimentation of the sixties, seventies and eighties is a lost cause. No one wants to go back to the conditions out of which such art emerged: the squats, the social experiments, and so forth. People now look enviously at Berlin, Warsaw, Vilnius, Istanbul, all those places where the scene is extremely lively. But they don't want the misery that generates such energy - it's like waking up when you could go on sleeping. It's called dreaming.

"Yes, I do feel responsible in a sense. My task is to be different. Difficult, provocative. Not stupid or sensational, but intelligent. The museum does not need to be a box office draw - that was never the purpose of museums. If the museum has to draw the public, we might as well become a McDonald's.

"That's not to say that the public isn't welcome. On the contrary. But I see the task of the museum in the city and in the region as like that of a power plant. You don't go there every week either, but it's needed to generate energy. It would be a brilliant political move for the government to change the mandate of museums and say 'You are not here to attract the public, you are here to increase the creative power in your area.'
Then the museum could start doing very different things, and probably with less money. Other jobs would arise. We would create work, using the collection as our energy supply.

"If the museum can function like that for its own region, I will be very satisfied. And if a new, lively artists' colony arises here, it will be good for the museum, for Eindhoven, for Brabant and ultimately for the Netherlands as well – but it must happen in that order, not the other way round."

Sacha Bronwasser is a freelance art journalist for the *Volkskrant* and *Vrij Nederland*. In addition, she gives lectures and conducts public interviews on topics concerning art and art-house film. She is regularly involved in the organization of exhibitions and festivals.

Tulips and Windmills Forever
From the Holland Brand to the Dutch Design Brand

Mention Holland and most people conjure up an image of tulips and windmills, dykes and polders, canals, quaint buildings, and the swirling brushstrokes of Vincent van Gogh. But you'd be hard pressed to find a Dutchman, let alone a designer, who would not scoff at such tired old clichés. They would tell you instead that the Netherlands is a markedly progressive country where plenty of others things are going on. And yet, it cannot be denied that these standard images tell a lot about our little kingdom. They stand for the artificial landscape that we have created here in the delta of the Rhine, as well as for the continual transformation of nature into artificial values – whether tulips or investments – that underlies the Dutch economy and culture. Tulips and windmills are indeed an entirely suitable 'brand image' for Holland.

Historical origins
—

Fortunately, some designers here know how to work with this brand. A broad range of products has won new ground for the brand Holland, whether it is through the recycling of traditional Delft blue decorative patterns in the work of Ineke Hans or Hella Jongerius, the continuation of Dutch forms of landscape and urbanism in the work of Adriaan Geuze, or the playing on the artificiality of our environment in the work of OMA, MVRDV, Maxwan or NL Architects. Together these experiments make up what we think of today as Dutch Design.
The historical origins of the current *succès d'estime* of Dutch design can be found in what talented people have made of the geography and location of this country, as well as in the policy decisions successive Dutch governments have made in the fields of art, architecture and design down all of the twentieth century. The Netherlands is largely a man-made country, of course, created in part by draining over 3000 polders and protected from the sea and rivers with dikes that are continually strengthened and heightened. From as long ago as the 17th century this country has also always had to depend upon derived value: we are primarily traders. Products made elsewhere are brokered here (an activity that is becoming increasingly virtual), and that which is produced here gains its value from the degree to which it is manipulated. Particularly in the agricultural sector – in animal breeding and plant manipulation, for example – one can discern an intense artificiality. Holland is a country that accepts the artificial as normal. The interest in the commonplace, and what can be done with it to create added value, has run through the arts here for centuries. It is indeed all about windmills and tulips, polders and canal houses – at least as far as image is concerned.
In the 20th century the Dutch developed a modern architecture and art and design, based upon its landscape, that transformed that reality into an abstract play of line and form. The paintings of Piet Mondrian and the designs of Gerrit Rietveld were central to this movement, and indeed, these two iconic figures still represent modern Holland to an art-conscious foreign public. This does not mean that their work was all that has happened here; many other styles and movements occurred, but modernism is characteristic – and that's what makes a brand.

These modern forms are supported by a particular methodology that has come to be called 'conceptual'. This is the process that connects the landscape to the economy and the arts. Collecting information and transforming it into a new reality that in its artificiality shows that information can be used not just to drive speculation, but also to create new forms, images and spaces. At work here is a simple, sober refusal to make something that rises out of the ordinary and instead to apply oneself to refining the commonplace. In this sense, the buildings of MVRDV are the equivalent of the hybrid tulip, and the chairs of Richard Hutten are miniature polders.

National design methodology

—

It is the government, which in history has commissioned the newest and largest polders and representative buildings such as cultural institutions, and the research that has been carried out by avid urban planners since Cornelis van Eesteren, that has made possible the development of Dutch design. On a smaller scale, the government has acted in the background as a supporter of this movement, encouraging the development of a variety of forms and images rather than favouring a few prestige buildings or artworks that could then supposedly increase public awareness. In Holland, it's a matter of religious and social "pillars" rather than of monumental columns, postage stamps rather than historic paintings, varying styles of social housing rather than national museums. One can find examples to belie this, naturally, but they are not always the most successful artworks, and not characteristic of this country. The Louvre is better than the Rijksmuseum, the Wibautstraat is no Champs-Elysées and there is no Dutch Géricault.
Commissioning of art and architecture in the Netherlands is splintered, divided not only between different ministries and government departments at the state, provincial and municipal levels, but also between the various institutions which have emerged from the old compartmentalisation of social, cultural and educational along religious and political lines. This fragmentation carries over into Dutch education in art, architecture and design. Not surprisingly, there is no national school or style. A national design methodology however does exist: it is a process that stems from the traditions and ways in which things are made here. Investigative designing, conceptual thinking, and the mirroring, mapping and refining of reality are the most important characteristics of the Holland brand when it comes to design – the brand we call Dutch Design.
And that brand has suddenly become popular. This is in part because a number of organizations emerged from the fragmented traditions of this field in the early 1990s to represent the brand with great power. The most important of these are Droog Design and Rem Koolhaas' Office for Metropolitan Architecture (OMA). They had predecessors in such national institutions as the NS Rail Service and the PTT Postal Service and in studios like Van den Broek en Bakema and Total Design, but there is one crucial difference: Droog and OMA not only concentrate much more consciously on Dutch Design, but do this primarily abroad.
As a result, something inherent in the way in which the Dutch give form to the landscape, the objects and the images of everyday life suddenly gained a visible and distinguishable reality, which, after the results were published and lauded abroad, could also be understood in Holland. Books like the Droog catalogues and the OMA manifestos certainly contributed to this situation, as did Hans Ibelings's *Kunstmatig Landschap*, Bart Lootsma's *Superdutch* and my own *False Flat*.

Government support

—

The government does support the Dutch Design brand. It does so both indirectly, making it possible for designers to work conceptually here and very directly through the subsidies for international presentations granted by the Mondriaan Foundation and the Netherlands Architecture Fund, by the events supported by the Ministry of Foreign Affairs, and through exhibitions like those that we of the Netherlands Architecture Institute organise for foreign venues.

I believe that this fragmentary approach is typically Dutch and crucial to the development of the Dutch Design brand. Precisely because there is no centralised control, an array of designers gets the chance to be promoted abroad; and it turns out that, on balance, their various efforts support the idea that there is a particular methodology – not a style – which is the Dutch contribution to the international discussion on design. Consciously working with the artificiality of our reality, thinking conceptually, the idea that design means the mapping, reflecting and refining of reality – these are all Dutch qualities that, in contrast to style, which is subject to fashion, can remain interesting over the long term and be applied at many different locations. The task of the Dutch government is both to sustain this attitude and process and to go on making it possible to present Dutch Design to the world.

In concrete terms, the Dutch government would do well to give decentralised and targeted support to the presentation of Dutch work abroad, but also to give Dutch designers the chance to demonstrate their methodology through workshops and lectures. Here the key is: the more varied, the better, while maintaining high standards.

There remain, however, two problems with this policy. First there is no clearly measurable economic result. Precisely because this design is about processes and concepts, the product is of secondary importance, so often enough there is nothing to sell. Any result that does emerge is shaped by the process, making it difficult to reproduce. If the government were to make a cost/benefit analysis of this policy, little of it would remain. The only other argument I can propose is that Dutch companies working abroad may profit by the innovative, experimental and even amusing aspects of the Dutch Design brand, but this would be difficult to prove.

The second problem is that a targeted and decentralised approach means that it is difficult to defend these subsidies and supportive measures against the inevitable rounds of budget cuts that are the order of the day in any modern economy. The Dutch design world has difficulty making a stand to save an institution or organization from increasingly deep "paring of the cheese slicer" (the Dutch method of successive cuts in subsidies) as that requires simultaneously lobbying the budgets of the Ministry of Education, Cultural Affairs and Science, the Ministry of Housing, Regional Development and the Environment, the Ministry of Transport and Public Works, the Ministry of Foreign Affairs, the Amsterdam and Rotterdam mayors and their city councils, and the all the various semi-independent foundations.

International perspective

—

Why should the government keep supporting the presentation of Dutch design abroad, and how can we ensure that it does? I think that the Netherlands can and should be proud of what it has developed in this field, and that Dutch Design can be used to create a distinct Dutch national profile. The establishment of this identity may not lead to a

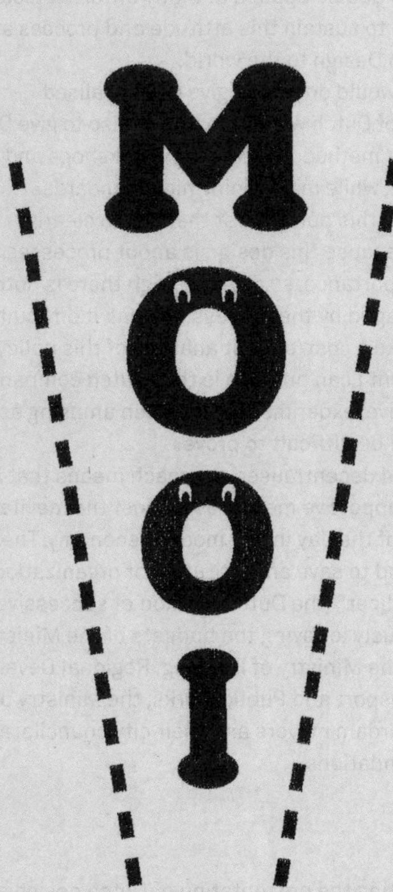

was the first Dutch word I have heard.
sounded friendly to me.

style – which is the Dutch contribution to the international
. Consciously working with the artificiality of our reality, thinking
a that design means the mapping, reflecting and refining of reality
qualities that, in contrast to style, which is subject to fashion,
ng over the long term and be applied at many different locations.
government is both to sustain this attitude and process and to
ible to present Dutch Design to the world.
e Dutch government would do well to give decentralised
to the presentation of Dutch work abroad, but also to give Dutch
to demonstrate their methodology through workshops and lectures.
ore varied, the better, while maintaining high standards.
er, two problems with this policy. First there is no clearly
ic result. Precisely because this design is about processes and
ct is of secondary importance, so often enough there is nothing
at does emerge is shaped by the process, making it difficult to
ernment were to make a cost/benefit analysis of this policy, little
he only other argument I can propose is that Dutch companies
profit by the innovative, experimental and even amusing aspects
brand, but this would be difficult to prove.
is that a targeted and decentralised approach means that it is
ese subsidies and supportive measures against the inevitable
ts that are the order of the day in any modern economy. The Dutch
ficulty making a stand to save an institution or organization from
aring of the cheese slicer" (the Dutch method of successive cuts
requires simultaneously lobbying the budgets of the Ministry of
Affairs and Science, the Ministry of Housing, Regional Development
t, the Ministry of Transport and Public Works, the Ministry of
Amsterdam and Rotterdam mayors and their city councils, and
mi-independent foundations.

ctive

rnment keep supporting the presentation of Dutch design abroad,
ure that it does? I think that the Netherlands can and should be
developed in this field, and that Dutch Design can be used to create
onal profile. The establishment of this identity may not lead to a

factories, but it does have designers who can remain in the world's t
because their conceptual approach can adapt to any circumstance.
of tulips to the State Secretary, fly a flag from your windmill: Dutch [
everything that is good, beautiful and charming about the Netherlan
around the world ought to know about that.

Aaron Betsky is the director of the Netherlands Architecture Institute. Also active as
his most recent book is *False Flat: Why Dutch Design is So Good* (2004). He writes
periodicals *Bouw* and *Man* and regularly gives lectures on architecture and design

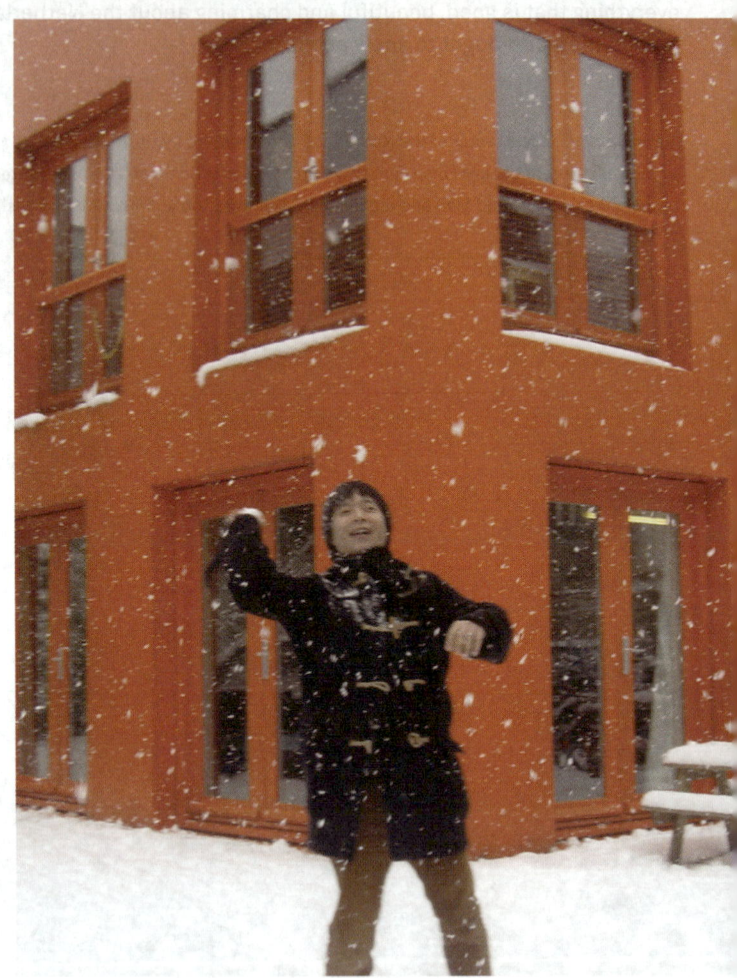

The image colour of the Netherlands is orange. Why do they like orange? Orange makes me feel cheerful, warm, fun, and gentle.

concrete economic result, but it will ensure that the Netherlands continues to exist as a country and a concept - and in a situation where borders and national currencies are disappearing, that's maybe not such a strange idea. Besides, the Netherlands is sure to remain pre-eminent in this field. Finally, it is also quite possible that in an increasingly internationally-oriented economy, this brand will prove to be important in the competition for commissions, attracting businesses, and generating employment opportunities. (The Premsela Dutch Design Foundation has submitted the economic argument to this effect for political discussion at the national level.)
It is necessary to put forth these arguments continually and in all sorts of different forums. Now it is up to all institutions and individuals in the field of design to persist in arguing for support of the Dutch Design brand abroad for conceptual reasons as well. The Netherlands may not be the country with the best scientists or the biggest factories, but it does have designers who can remain in the world's top rank precisely because their conceptual approach can adapt to any circumstance. Send a bouquet of tulips to the State Secretary, fly a flag from your windmill: Dutch Design stands for everything that is good, beautiful and charming about the Netherlands, and people all around the world ought to know about that.

Aaron Betsky is the director of the Netherlands Architecture Institute. Also active as a writer and publicist, his most recent book is *False Flat: Why Dutch Design is So Good* (2004). He writes monthly columns for the periodicals *Bouw* and *Man* and regularly gives lectures on architecture and design.

A Plea for More Cultural Institutes Abroad
Bert van Meggelen interviewed by *Sandra Jongenelen*

The Netherlands should substantially increase the number of its cultural institutes abroad. There is the Institut Néerlandais in Paris, Jakarta has its Erasmushuis, and in Brussels the Vlaams-Nederlands Huis recently opened its doors. But those are not nearly enough.

"There should be ten or fifteen such institutions around the world," says Bert van Meggelen (58), originally a sociologist and the founder of Stichting Maatwerk, an agency specialising in urban development and cultural planning. As its director, he gives advice on projects such as the refurbishment of the Grote Markt in Groningen, where he was asked to come up with a plan to make the eastern side of that open-air market culturally attractive.

After completing a study specialised in housing and planning, Van Meggelen worked for almost 20 years in the field of architectural education, including holding a position as director of the Academy of Architecture and Urban Planning, RAG (Rotterdam, Arnhem and Groningen). At the turn of the millennium his knowledge of art and culture was bolstered by his appointment to the directorship of Stichting R2001, Rotterdam Cultural Capital.

A cultural institute is a valuable tool for keeping the world up-to-date on Dutch art and culture, he feels. "We need places for collaboration, not more cultural attachés. An institute can keep track of interesting developments abroad, it can bring in Dutch people and, most importantly, provide contacts. Cultural attachés, like those we now have in New York and Berlin, are not solely the answer. They should act as trailblazers for our institutes."

Van Meggelen cites Sabine Henzsch's approach to directing the Goethe Institute in Rotterdam as a useful example. "Henzsch did not say, 'Germany has quite a lot of charming things', but instead asked herself how she could make a contribution to art and culture in the guest country itself. So it's not only about promoting German culture, but also about how German artists can contribute to the Dutch situation."

By boosting the number of its institutes, the Netherlands can help build a Cultural Europe. "While Europe is a monetary, agricultural and economic project, its cultural aspect seems non-existent. Europe's success will depend on culture." On the economic and monetary level, it was the eradication of differences that made the common market possible, explains Van Meggelen. In Europe, bananas must be curved in a certain way to be allowed into the market, and thanks to the common currency, banking transactions are no longer impeded by the necessity of changing into and out of so many different currencies. "With culture, however, it's not about eradicating differences, but articulating them. We're proud of precisely what distinguishes us from our neighbours, rather than what we have in common. We should celebrate our differences. That's an interesting point, certainly in a world where difference is considered frightening."

But before establishing cultural institutes in other countries, perhaps we should examine whether Dutch culture *needs* to be visible in the rest of the world. And if it does, should that be more than simply as a summation of individual artists and art institutions? In both cases van Meggelen's response is affirmative. "We have a lot to offer. Because art and culture presumes both similarities and differences in values there is a certain spin-off from international cultural policy to other areas of society, for instance politics and law, or economics and agriculture. Being proud of Dutch culture and presenting it on a larger, international scale is both a way of expressing that pride and an attempt to match our own culture with those of others, accentuating it and putting it into perspective."

Next year the Netherlands celebrates the 400th anniversary of the birth of its most famous painter. Should the Dutch promote 'Rembrandt Year' on an international cultural level? Yes and no, says Van Meggelen diplomatically. "If the only purpose of Rembrandt Year is to promote tourism, I don't think it's worthwhile. It should involve more than fossilised heritage. A better question would be: Can Rembrandt lead to anything in the future? And if so, what? What's the artistic, cultural or social significance of Rembrandt Year? If you can answer that, then it's interesting. Otherwise not. There's nothing wrong with hype for tourists, but from a cultural point of view it's meaningless."
Foreign cultural policy is made to a great degree by the Ministry of Foreign Affairs. There is a hidden danger here, according to Van Meggelen. "Art and culture must not be used to jazz something else up. They are too valuable for that. But at the same time, the arts can play a meaningful role in other sectors, for example in environmental planning and safety."
"Art is always about art, of course, and that's interesting for the arts, just as a writer who primarily writes for other writers is interesting for literature. But art is always produced within a context, from which various meanings can be deduced. To give an example: One of the great problems of our time is fear. People are afraid of change; they're quivering with uncertainty. As a remedy we have insurance companies, but we have to learn to live with the unexpected. Art can teach us how.
By radicalising, denying or ridiculing other people's fears, we can reduce our own fear and put it into perspective."
Although this is a subject that invites further investigation, it does not seem to be a big issue among Dutch artists and producers. "The situation is very different in France, and in Germany, which has the philosopher Sloterdijk, and where the writer Heinrich Böll was more or less the conscience of the nation. Whenever something major happens in Germany, you see artists and intellectuals reacting on television. That doesn't happen in the Netherlands."

How outsiders see the Netherlands depends on which discipline is involved. "If you look at international art events like Documenta, where the artists are selected by an international curator, then the Dutch tend to be under- rather than over-represented. But if you attend an architectural biennial, it's packed with Dutch exhibits. That's partly due to Koolhass and the internationally famous architects in his slipstream. Something similar holds true for design. We're world champions in that as well."
Across the border, Dutch architecture is hot. "Here in the Netherlands, exhibitions of the work of Dutch architects usually draw a few people from the press, some architecture junkies and a handful of ordinary people." There was a presentation in the Czech Republic recently. "The interest was tremendous – people came in droves. You see the same thing with the press. Foreign newspapers carry far more articles about Dutch architecture than our own do."
Whether or not the world has a positive view of Dutch culture is partly a matter of

personal opinion – and for Van Meggelen this is a plus, because you can influence opinions. "For example, you can have cultural representatives meet with the editors of papers like Die Zeit, El Pais, Le Monde and The Guardian. We did that for Rotterdam Cultural Capital of Europe, with very pleasing results."
How the Netherlands is seen depends to some extent on the political persuasion of the foreigner concerned. "Conservatives generally have an image of a heroin-shooting, whore-hopping nation that murders unborn babies and senior citizens. Those who are more interested in experiment see a progressive country whose citizens have casual, almost brazen manners, very different from the formality and grandeur of the French."
What Van Meggelen himself considers typical for the Netherlands is the large number of foreigners holding top positions in the cultural sector. The directors of the Netherlands Architecture Institute, the Van Gogh Museum, the Van Abbemuseum, the Dutch National Opera, the Holland Festival, and until recently the Rotterdam Film Festival and the Dutch National Ballet are all foreigners. The same is true of the chief conductors of the Rotterdam Philharmonic Orchestra and the Royal Concertgebouw Orchestra.
Van Meggelen: "In Paris, you see only French people at the top; in Belgium there's not a single foreigner to be found; and in Germany, too, it's awfully hard to find a Dutch person in a prominent cultural position. I'm not arguing in favour of foreigners, but the idea that the top positions in the Netherlands don't necessarily have to be occupied by Dutch people does have some merit. It keeps the recruiting possibilities broad. What's more, foreigners can function as ambassadors for the Netherlands in their home countries."
What is also striking about the Netherlands is how often you hear the words 'modernisation' and 'innovation'. "It's a pity for tradition, because the emphasis is on staying up-to-the-minute. That's why fast moving, hype-oriented disciplines like design and photography do so well." The focus on innovation is a given in Dutch history. "Rembrandt, Van Gogh, and Mondrian were all innovators. And in this century, Koolhaas." The Netherlands would do well to promote its innovative cultural elan more aggressively. Van Meggelen: "It's ridiculous that 'Holland promotion' still focuses on tulips and clogs. If you want to show that the Netherlands is a forward looking, innovative nation, you can't keep coming up with windmills and cheese. Mondrian might be too complicated, Van Gogh too much of a cliché, but perhaps Ben van Berkel's bridge over the river Maas in Rotterdam is an option. The bridge is more than just infrastructure, more than a link between A and B. It's an artwork over water, a marriage of art and technology. It refers to the Dutch iconic struggle with water and it also forms a link between the 'poor' and 'less poor' sections of the city. But Van Meggelen doubts whether Van Berkel's bridge will ever become a Dutch trademark. "The problem of choosing a trademark for the Netherlands would probably degenerate into another football match."

Sandra Jongenelen is a freelance journalist for *Het Financieele Dagblad* and *Kunstbeeld*, and a member of the advisory council for *Boekman*, a journal for art, culture and policy.

Culture as Dynamic

Prologue
—

A brief autobiographical introduction: I make my living in the cultural sector,
where I busy myself with the dual – and sometimes competing – tasks of analysis and
reproduction. The former task covers any number of historically and culturally specific
explorations of how people deploy, negotiate, and use a wide range of media and it
includes, most recently, a five-year investigation into media and identity in Europe.[1]
The latter task entails teaching, and I work in university programs on both sides of
the Atlantic, brokering the insights of the past and interrogating the experiences of
the present in order to shape the creators and critics of tomorrow, hoping to spark in
them a sense of curiosity, of implication, and perspective. These tasks collide when the
analytic project risks consuming the project of reproduction, dissecting it with critical
gusto. Thinking about how and why cultural practices have emerged and witnessing
the fabric of assumptions from radically divergent viewpoints, tends to destabilize
(if not dissolve) the object of reproduction. And so it is with this essay. There are good
reasons to think carefully about concepts that seem almost naturally to bind our
experience and define our institutional practices; but if we press too hard, we risk
dissolving the very categories that we seek to understand. I am aware of this danger,
and proceed with the hope that should this occur, at least we might see other ways to
formulate our questions.

If Delft blue windmills, wooden shoes, and kissing figurines in national costume still
fill the shelves of Dutch souvenir shops, they do so in a very different identity context
than even ten years ago. Leaving aside the problem of competing claims on these
icons (Copenhagen's souvenir shops are full of the identical Chinese-made objects),
long held assumptions about Dutchness and the identity of the nation are currently
subject to dispute. Creating pressure from the inside, major populations in cities such
as Amsterdam and Rotterdam are no longer white or Christian or speak Dutch as a
first language. Dutch cuisine has been relegated to a tourist speciality in a culinary
landscape dominated by Italian, Chinese, French, and American fast food restaurants.
From the outside, Europe – itself in the throes of an identity crisis as it assimilates
new nations and struggles to establish a constitution and sensible work regime
– poses challenges in areas until recently held to be the domain of the Dutch state.
Deprived of its culturally distinctive paper currency, facing regulatory incursions into
long established agricultural practices, and witnessing the 'Europeanization' of its
education system thanks to the Treaty of Bologna (in which 29 European nations agreed
to reform their systems of higher education), it seems that the state can no any longer
take anything for granted. Against this background, the recent debates provoked by the
very un-Dutch political assassinations of politician Pim Fortuyn and film director and
columnist Theo van Gogh have triggered attempts to formulate and define the nation
and its values for all of those who would be a part of it. One way of thinking about
efforts to reconsider, renew and possibly re-brand Dutch Culture (with a capital 'C') is to
see it as part of this initiative, a counter offensive seeking to reclaim an identity under

siege. Yet, at a moment when even Dutch concerns such as Philips and increasingly the flower business are shifting their operations out of the Netherlands, and as incursions from inside and out seem to redouble their intensity, the success of such initiatives seems questionable.

Culture & culture
—

While these changes have certainly provoked a sense of uncertainty as well as valiant attempts to fight back and assert national tradition, both changes and reactions need to be seen against the much larger backdrop of history and language, against a texture of everyday life that has marked and defined the culture over the long term. From this perspective, the latest transformations seem nor more than a blip in a long and illustrious tradition. But that tradition is itself dynamic, with the Netherlands as a physical territory and Dutch as a language, demonstrating remarkable fluidity over the course of time. Fluid or not, and this is Hobsbawm and Ranger's point,[2] there is a core of accepted traditions and fictions that help to stabilize and centre the dynamic edges of a nation, and the Netherlands is no exception. It is no accident that the time when the Dutch were active in exploring and colonizing the world, transforming the identities of the many cultures they encountered, was also the time that we can most easily point to as a golden age, when brand-Nederland was easy to recognize in painting, for example. And today, when the nation is on the receiving as well as the giving end of the many dynamics wrapped up in the term 'globalization', it is also no wonder that its identity is increasingly blurred.

If by culture we mean those collective behaviours and products of a people studied by anthropologists, two things are certain. First, Dutch culture is alive and well, linked by history and genealogy through generations of evolving and accreting practices, and stabilized by whatever national framework we decide to impose upon it. Second, it is an emphatically plural culture – or perhaps better, a multitude of intertwined cultures, organized along the fault lines of taste, region, ethnicity, age and gender. Each of these has a schizophrenic relationship to the project of nationhood, at once helping to constitute it and reaching outwards across national boundaries, enacting the terms of cultural (as opposed to national) specificity by aligning with trans-national cohorts. Dutch lovers of early Renaissance music may have more in common with their French or Belgian counterparts than with fellow countrymen who are Britney Spears fans. Cultural citizenship does not necessarily coincide with national borders. But if by culture we mean Culture, that is, a limited domain of expressive practices and institutions – music, painting, architecture, literature, theatre, television, film, etc. – we enter a rarefied world of critics, taste-makers, investors, policy makers, and often (depending on the cultural form) state subsidized museums, publishers, concert halls, etc. This kind of culture is far less organic than the anthropological sort, and far more subject to the interests, pressures, and discourses of various elites – both national and international. Culture, in this sense, and as described to us by sociologists from Becker to Bourdieu,[3] is closely related to notions of taste, to structures of cultural power and strategies for social distinction. Although garbed in concepts of truth and beauty, its mechanisms, strict hierarchies, and patterns of social deployment suggest that something far more mundane is at work. A sub-category of culture, Culture can be aesthetically profound and moving, but it is inseparable from an agenda that focuses on distinction – a context-dependent term that could refer to social position, or to nation, or to trans-national taste-cohorts, but always turns on identity.

Identities

—

Because *in situ* identity is always pluralform, I prefer to use the term identities. Identities tend to be dynamic and relative. They are dynamic in the sense that they change in response to different situations and appeals (in certain settings, our gender identity may supersede our national or occupational identities). And they are relative in the sense of being context-bound (a Dutch subject visiting the US is likely to be European; but in Europe, Dutch; and in the Netherlands, an Amsterdammer). Dutchness may also be triggered at home by transnational contexts: the Eurovision Song Contest, or world cup football, or even by the occasional war, national disaster or national holiday. Plural, dynamic, and relative, identities map onto the various collectivities that we participate in, and thus enjoy different levels of recognition and respect. One's identity as the subject of a nation is manifest in a documentary trail and regulated by the force of the state; one's identity as a participant in illegal music exchange systems is wholly voluntary, enacted through music file sharing, and till recently technically at odds with the rules of the nation. Most of us can negotiate the complicated demands of our various identities, and sometimes we even use one identity to camouflage another. These attributes of 'identity' when sited in humans also seem to hold when sited in non-human entities – cars, institutions, and even nations. With the key difference that they are discursively imposed rather than felt, the identities associated with nation can range from the declared (constitutions) to the hoped for (an immigrant's dreams), from the overtly iconic (wooden shoes and tolerance) to that which is actively repressed (nationalism).

The combination of identity and Culture may be as straightforward as the process of distinction just alluded to, or may emerge as something iconic and aspirational. If we pull the term nation (as a necessary fiction) into the mix, we may even have the makings of a branding strategy. Like the Nike swoosh trademark, iconic national Culture carries associations that are immediately evident; they link the familiar (the reified high points of Culture past) with the desired (our aspirations as a national culture), using a kind of shorthand that thrives on the specificity of reference and the ambiguity of meaning.

Media

—

Do some expressive forms, some modalities of Culture, relate to the project of nation and national identity more than others? This is a tricky question to answer, but there are grounds for suggesting that they do. Historically, and through the processes described by Hobsbawm and Ranger, some forms, 18th century Dutch painting is one example, have been closely associated with a richly developed national culture, with the project of national expansionism, and with the period's hierarchization of nations. If we think more in terms of the present, it seems that other forms, particularly those involving language (literature, theatre, film, broadcasting media, song), may be particularly apt carriers of national and popular memory and experience. The visual, spatial, and musical arts are obviously capable of this task as well, but the overlay of language and nation in these other forms gives them undoubted potential.[4] These distinctions are complicated by the social organization of Culture, and within living memory, that organization has changed profoundly. Before the widespread democratization of political voice and means of public expression associated with the 20th century (when women could finally vote and media such as film, low cost printing, and broadcasting opened up new communication channels), the Netherlands saw a relatively close correlation between Cultural elites and economic and political elites, and thus a close fit between Culture and nation. But the unfolding of the 20th century introduced new patterns, uncoupling the links between these three realms. Particularly after the Second World War, Culture continued to be guided and stimulated by the nation (subsidy), but its relevance was increasingly determined by the marketplace.

The explicit repositioning of Culture as market meant that artists in search of an international career had to depend more on individual marketing – and thus appeals to a trans-national taste cohort – than on association with a particular nation and its taste elites. Here, the non-language-based arts, unencumbered by the complications of translation, enjoy ease of access to trans-national markets. The shift to Culture as marketplace also meant that the public could vote with its feet, choosing trans-national Culture or Dutch Culture, increasing the divide between nation and Culture. In this context, medium specificity emerges as more important than ever. The film medium, for example, has been so long dominated by Hollywood that even in the Netherlands, Hollywood stands as a vernacular against which Dutch film appears as something exotic or exceptional. So, too, popular song. So how have language-based media been able to fight back? Perhaps the answer isn't to be found in the text, in the work itself, so much as in the format. Here, the principal of pluriformity behind the *Nederlands Omroepbestel* might be seen as a resonant example. Not only is the policy unique, it reflects a unique sense of nation as a composite of distinct voices rather than a top-down imposition of homogenized imagery. That domestic television production, like the other language-based arts, helps to construct the nation's experience, serves as a repository of aspects of the national memory, and speaks in the national tongue, only reinforces its embrace of nation.

What next?

—

Subsidies remain the most effective way for a collective to ensure control over its representation. But as the logic of the neo-liberal state facilitates the project of global flows, we must attend carefully to the question of whose Culture is being sustained. We remain in the shadow of a Cultural system dominated by an aristocracy of taste; it is embedded in our history and our institutions, and it enjoys the advantage of being taken for granted. But as our cultural mix changes thanks to shifting populations, a changing European environment, and a re-definition of Culture as commodity, how should our subsidy system respond? Should we re-define the margins, shifting from the support of those with 'good taste' to those newcomers with distinctive cultural needs? Should we embrace the popular, hoping to engage larger publics? Should we support the work of language and memory – and the project of 'national identity' – developing new criteria for collective support? Should we focus on the structure of the Cultural, underscoring the centrality of concepts such as pluriformity in defining Dutch national identity, and supporting the channels necessary to make it flourish? Or should we redouble our efforts to deploy Culture as a national icon, making it the aesthetic equivalent of Delft blue windmills, wooden shoes, and kissing figurines in national costume, a floating signifier that smoothes over underlying diversity and difference?

The answer will not be easy. As we enter the 21st Century, and the old links between nation and taste continue to weaken, the implications of how we ask the question will continue to grow.

William Uricchio is professor and head of Comparative Media Studies at MIT and professor of Comparative Media History at Utrecht University in the Netherlands. A Guggenheim, Humboldt and Fulbright Fellow, his research considers the transformation of media technologies into media practices, in particular their role in (re-)constructing representation, knowledge and publics.

1 - The European Science Foundation program was entitled *Changing Media, Changing Europe*, and the project I led within it was 'Media and Identity: Homogenization and Diversity.'
2 - Eric Hobsbawm and Terence Ranger, *The Invention of Tradition* (Cambridge, 1983)
3 - Howard S. Becker, *Art Worlds* (Berkeley, 1982) and Pierre Bourdieu, *Distinction: A Social Critique of the Judgement of Taste* (Cambridge, MA, 1984)
4 - This sidesteps the problem of translation, whether of words or program formats, in which the foreign is localized. Still, the trace of national language invariably reinforces one dimension of nation.

Bring in the Cultivators

Jan Debbaut interviewed by *Sacha Bronwasser*

A modest room in an old building behind Tate Britain. A rug the colour of anthracite, two tables and a phone, three drawings by René Daniels on the wall. Jan Debbaut, Director of Collections at the Tate Gallery in London since 2003, feels at home here. Two acquisitions a day and a worldwide reputation to uphold means working hard, thinking big, spending grandly and at the same time keeping a tight grip on the purse strings. Everything is one size bigger, no, many sizes bigger than he was accustomed to in the Netherlands. "The Tate is a Ferrari. Step on the gas and you're doing 140. No more pleasantly puttering along, and at times that can be a disadvantage."
For fourteen years Debbaut was Director of the Van Abbemuseum in Eindhoven. Now that he no longer works in the Netherlands, he sees from a distance that the country scarcely plays any role in the world as a cultural entity. Can something be done about this? Debbaut's recommendations are replete with outlines, agenda items, and a three-step plan (perhaps that ought to have been four, he says, arms flailing). "The world has changed. The question is whether the Netherlands wants to change along with it."

"The way the Netherlands thinks the rest of the world perceives it does not accord with reality. I can see this more clearly now that I've been away for a while. I was biased too. When I worked in Eindhoven, I thought Dutch art and the Dutch art scene were of worldwide significance.
I realised this was not true when the tug-of-war over the Stedelijk Museum occurred. The museum imploded (figuratively), and nothing happened at all any more. I thought: surely the world will take notice and protest? But that didn't happen. For the outside world, the Stedelijk has ceased to exist. It can be reinstated, but really, nobody across the border cares very much.
Another example: I recently saw a splendid Stanley Brouwn exhibition in the Van Abbemuseum. And then when I returned to London, I discovered nobody had ever heard of him! No inkling of him at all! To my mind he was, and is, an important Dutch artist. But not elsewhere. In the Tate collections there are virtually no Dutch artists. My associates travel to Berlin, Warsaw, Madrid, St. Petersburg – but not to the Netherlands. The fact that we in the Netherlands are not even aware of this stems from a typically Dutch trait: we overestimate ourselves.

"The call for a distinct cultural profile for the Netherlands is based on a very different, but also very Dutch, idea: manipulability. That is an illusion. People think that as long as we have enough money and disburse it such and so, everything will work out fine. It's more complicated than that, however.
Three different factors are involved. The first is not in our hands: How good or bad is the art that is being produced? The second factor we *can* influence: What's the distribution system? How do the museums, the galleries, the auction houses and the art fairs function? And third: What's communication like? This means not only publicity and art criticism, but also guest curators, freelancers who work in a spread of countries and exchange information. How do we ensure that such people know about us?
Though the cultural image, or cultural profile, of the Netherlands is not manipulable,

the conditions for becoming acquainted with Dutch art in the first place are. They can
be improved. That's the place to start.

"As regards the first factor, Dutch art is no better or worse than art anywhere else;
as a matter of fact, sometimes it is very good. Marijke van Warmerdam, Edwin
Zwakman, Joep van Lieshout and de Rijke de Rooij, for example. To my delight, I see
younger artists getting around more, taking risks, operating internationally. A healthy,
emancipated, modern attitude is emerging. Fine work. But the important question is
what will be done with it. Let me put it this way: the fact that the goods are not on the
shelf does not mean that they are bad. It's simply that nobody knows they exist.

"My criticism has to do with the second factor; distribution through museums and the
commercial circuit. Museums should do coproductions, make exchanges, work together.
This is how affiliations based on trust arise. At the moment the Netherlands lacks that
kind of co-operation. What once was a network of reciprocity has gone. Then there
are the galleries, the dealers, the auction houses. This sector is focused on the home
market, and is not expansion-oriented. A case in point: the work of Marlene Dumas is
currently a worldwide success, but her gallery in Antwerp (Zeno X) works harder than
her Dutch gallery.
Look at it this way: assuming that I (like so many others) do *not* visit the Netherlands,
how can I stay informed? I could attend the big international fairs, but far too few
Dutch gallery holders participate in such events. This has to do with the limited number
of collectors in the Netherlands. They are very few, and they do not actively make
themselves known. Here in the Tate alone I deal with 100, maybe 150 collectors.
Take Belgium – collectors are the mainstay of that country. I miss this social factor
in the Netherlands, where there are maybe ten collectors to another country's 200.
Has the Netherlands ever asked itself why there are so few collectors? Given the
prodigious amounts of money that have been made in the Netherlands in recent years,
if there were the same tax deductions that other countries allow for the non-profit
sector you'd be amazed at how much money would start flowing! If I could have offered
a tax break when I was in the Eindhoven area, where there are a lot of entrepreneurs,
I could have put together very different exhibitions. And as far as possible, I did.
I had the first sponsor's club in the Netherlands; my whole acquisition policy there
was financed by private parties. And let's not forget the Mondriaan Foundation.

"Then the third factor. There's a worldwide circuit, or actually several circuits, of good
publicists and guest curators who very deliberately take 'their' artists with them.
Such talented people, sharing information on the circuit, dream up new events. But
I see very few Dutch people among them. And how can those decision-makers abroad
do anything with Dutch art if they hear so little about it?
We need to invest in these people. Invite them in and let them choose. Don't say:
I've put together a wonderful exhibition; would your museum in Chicago like to have it?
Any self-respecting curator will say: thanks, but that's not my own selection. So bring
that man or woman from Chicago to the Netherlands and say: how would you like to do
it? If you're not familiar with the art here, come and take a look at our expense.
Invest in their interest. There is plenty of seed potential in the Netherlands. You have
to bring in the cultivators. Not the retailers! Art is not like cheese or tulip bulbs. You
can't export it.

I organized the Netherlands' exhibit for the Venice Biennale twice. On both occasions I spent more time figuring out the lists of Dutch guests for the Dutch dinner and smoothing the ruffled feathers this aroused than I did thinking: *Where are the most important critics, the press, the collectors?* Why didn't I sit at the table of Barbara Gladstone who might have been willing to give one of our artists an exhibition? There was neither the time nor the means for it; people didn't consider such things important. After all, it was primarily a pleasant outing, wasn't it? But you're there at a fair, darn it, you're there to sell your product.

"The world has changed, and the question is whether the Netherlands, at the moment relegated to the periphery, is going to become part of it again. You can choose to emulate the big players, whose museums no longer do their own publicity. They outsource it to the top professional agencies, of which there are only a few in the world. Everybody hires them – except the Dutch. It costs a lot of money, but you can count on attention, the proper writers, and worldwide media coverage. The money has to come from somewhere. Your museums must get into branding, perhaps even franchising. The Tate Gallery receives fully a third of its income from commercial activities and is setting up branches in Latin America, China and Eastern Europe. Is this possible or even desirable in the Netherlands? Perhaps a better way for the Dutch is not to conform, but to look for niches – areas where the big players are not yet active. I'll give another example from the Van Abbemuseum because I happen to know it so well: I think it's clever of Charles Esche, my successor, not to even attempt to compete with the big museums like the Tate or MoMa. As a small museum, he has aligned himself with the Istanbul Biennale and, very wisely, involves all of his staff in the project. From there, the hinterlands of the Middle East and beyond are open to him, and that is today's Silk Route. Through his museum, he is building up knowledge of an area that is yet to be exploited. And look at Rem Koolhaas – he too has created a niche, a wondrous terrain of architecture, urban culture, design, photography and more. His work has generated enormous interest, attracting adherents, and has become an international phenomenon. Searching for niches can be a good strategy. Subsidies in the Netherlands must be distributed in a better way: instead of spreading resources out over all those institutions and applicants we should invest in the proverbial mad genius with a good plan – even with the risk of getting the paint scratched or that something explodes. Anything's better than money being nicely, controllably, sustainably and equitably distributed, but leaving the art unseen."

Sacha Bronwasser is a freelance art journalist for the *Volkskrant* and *Vrij Nederland*. In addition, she gives lectures and conducts public interviews on topics concerning art and art-house film. She is regularly involved in the organization of exhibitions and festivals.

Culture and Politics

Mutual Engagement

The editorial in the *Volkskrant* of 27 November 2004 was entirely given over to 'Politics and Art'. This was unique, so I cut it out and saved it. The immediate occasion was the discussion in the Lower House on the cultural budget that week, which produced the by-now familiar "pathetic spectacle" in which "art institutions demean themselves by shamelessly begging for funds and lobbying politicians, who in turn cannot resist acting like Santa Claus, handing out presents that reward the best beggar's act, rather than the greatest artistic accomplishment."
This four-yearly spectacle "not only undermines the credibility of politicians, but that of the art world itself," according to the editors. Strong language this, followed by two bold recommendations: "In the first place, create a separate system with longer-running subsidy cycles for large, nationally important art institutions such as the Rijksmuseum and the Dutch National Opera. For the smaller ones, establish a financial threshold, whatever form that may take. Secondly, keep politics further removed from art. The British Arts Council is a good example. It allocates subsidies independently; the government simply checks up afterwards."

The first recommendation amounts to a good pragmatic solution for a problem which is above all practical. The relationship between art and politics will not change substantially because of it. The second is an example of a typically Dutch conditioned reflex: The relationship between art and politics is no good, so let's increase the distance between them. Leaving aside the question of whether such a great distance is typical of the Arts Council in Britain, which I doubt, isn't the proposed solution precisely the problem? Isn't there in fact too great a distance between the two? Wouldn't it be better if artists were more intensively involved with politically important themes and politicians had a more intensive relationship with the arts? Wouldn't this be more likely to eliminate our 'pathetic' reflexive behaviour?
Lately, in spite of the views of liberal politician Thorbecke, that politicians have no business interfering in the content of art, these questions are being posed more often. Not just in regard to the Netherlands' national arts policy, but also to our international policy on arts and culture. An international outlook is precisely what is needed to prompt artists and policymakers to question the commonly accepted dogma of (too much) mutual distance.

For Els van der Plas, director of the Prince Claus Foundation, culture and politics are inseparable. She has experienced this directly through projects and awards for artists in 'difficult countries' in Africa, Asia and the Middle East. Acting as an 'Amnesty' for culture, the Foundation supports oppressed artists in these countries in an effort to call the world's attention to their work — which always involves a pronounced engagement with their own culture — and simultaneously to call attention to the distressing political situation in their countries. The quality of the work must always come first, according to Van der Plas, but when it comes to choosing between works of acceptable quality, what tips the balance is the engagement of the artist.
The policy of the Prince Claus Foundation is to interweave art and politics. It makes

no bones about this. Yet speaking from experience, Van der Plas emphasizes that she is 'hesitant' about employing culture purely as a remedy in a political situation, and she warns against having unrealistic expectations of the political effect of intercultural dialogue – although it must certainly continue, nonetheless.

Dragan Klaic is capable of having an intercultural dialogue *with himself,* since he is a cosmopolitan of the old guard, as it were. Born and raised in former Yugoslavia (Belgrade, Serbia), educated at Harvard and since the outbreak of the civil war in the early nineties resident and working in the Netherlands – he was until a few years ago director of the Theater Instituut Nederland, and Professor of Theatre Science in Amsterdam.
No wonder, then, that in his essay he ends up advocating the pursuit of a European cultural identity – as an antidote, that is, to the resurgent desire for a national identity. Since the '*Wende*', we have become used to this nostalgic tendency in the former Central and East European countries, but now the Netherlands itself is pervaded with national-historic, literary-scientific and cultural canons that purportedly give us (back) our national identity. For any soul who's the least bit nomadic – as most artists are – this is a rather unattractive, if not frightening development.
The active promotion of a European cultural identity (a 'unity in diversity', naturally) must be championed, paradoxically enough, by these same national states – because the member states, including the original ones, are particularly devoted to the principal of subsidiarity, meaning that anything that can be done at the national level must not be handed over to Brussels. This has produced a lousy cultural policy at the European level. Until now.

If the chairman of the European Commission, the Portuguese Barroso, has anything to do with it, this will change. During a meeting sponsored by the Dutch government during the Dutch presidency of the European Union and organized by Nexus, he stated that as far as he is concerned culture is more important for Europe than economics. Truly a statement people will remember and try to hold him to!
I heard him say it again on television, in the VPRO documentary *Thinking about Europe* by Jos de Putter. Sure enough, in the first sentence of his contribution to this book, De Putter stipulates: "Culture is back on the political agenda." According to De Putter, art in the (post)modern era has allowed itself to be confined in a ghetto by politics. And art – being all too autonomous and 'lured away' from other areas of life such as the economy and politics – has helped confine itself to that ghetto.
What we have experienced in the past few years is a fairly hard-headed confrontation between art as the autonomously 'beautiful' and art as the 'morally good'. A new balance must be found between them, De Putter maintains. But in doing so, art must not become any less controversial, for this is one of its most important characteristics. Inspired by the German Islamist Bassam Tibi and by young Eastern European architects, Jos de Putter goes on to make an impassioned plea for the designing of new cultural spaces in Europe, particularly in the mass media and in what we now call public space. He places the emphasis not on the market and politics, but on the cultural dimension of Europe, enthusiastically defending and articulating what the politician Barroso may perhaps have said without giving it too much thought.

It is common knowledge that the politician Boris Dittrich advocates an art policy that will guarantee the autonomy of the arts. He takes the same position with regard to

Introduction by Ben Hurkmans

international cultural policy. Accordingly, he believes in a policy which strengthens the quality of culture, recognizes the intrinsic value of art and supports initiatives which come from that sector. Does this mean Dittrich would send the arts back to the ghetto of the 'autonomously beautiful' from which De Putter wants to free them? Not really, since he does acknowledge two other objectives of international cultural policy – Holland Promotion and building bridges between cultures – whose nature is cultural-political rather than intrinsically artistic.

In order to resolve the tension created when these seemingly contrary objectives are brought together, Dittrich the politician comes up with concrete proposals. First of all, he recommends that cultural attachés be given their mandate not by the ministry but by a public national founding body, which after all works 'primarily for the cultural interest.' To support this recommendation, Dittrich refers to the well-known difference of opinion between the ministries of Foreign Affairs (culture as lubrication for international relations) and Cultural Affairs plus sundry public national founding bodies as detached posts, as regards their role as cultural advocates. That difference of opinion has long been a fiction, in so far as it ever existed at all. All the same, operating in a less governmental fashion can be more effective in some regions and countries. The obvious solution is not to be part of an embassy or consulate, but to function independently as an art agency. This model has been very successfully adopted by, for example, the Swiss 'arts council' Pro Helvetia.

I believe that choosing this model should not lead to an increased distance between national politics and strategic choices in international cultural policy. On the contrary. At a strategic cultural/political level, the government can assume its responsibilities more effectively and thoroughly if we make the implementation of some sections of international cultural policy more non-governmental. The cultural debate in the parliament can only be improved by this

Referring to the *Institut du Monde Arabe* in Paris, Dittrich advocates an intensification of cultural ties with Turkey and Morocco, countries of origin for many people in the Netherlands. He also sees a role here for the European Union and feels that the EU cultural budget can and must be drastically increased.

With the 'Contemporary Arab Representations' series of exhibitions, Catherine David, former director of Witte de With, would appear to be operating at the cutting edge between art and politics. Perhaps that is why she articulates what art and what politics mean to her in such a trenchant manner.

For David, every work of art is political as well as aesthetic. "It's about defining standpoints and possibilities, which may give rise to conflicting interpretations." She quotes the French philosopher Jacques Rancière, who takes an extremely subtle view of the relationship between politics and art: "Art is not political because of the messages and feelings that it carries on the state of social and political issues. It is not political because of the way it represents social structures, conflicts or identities. It is political by virtue of the very distance that it takes from those functions." In this light, art is political, just as politics is an art. "There is an aesthetic dimension immanent to politics."

It is in concurrence with this view that I would argue for a more intensive reciprocal involvement of artists and politicians in the real world, each working from their own disciplines. They have more to offer each other than the relative mutual indifference

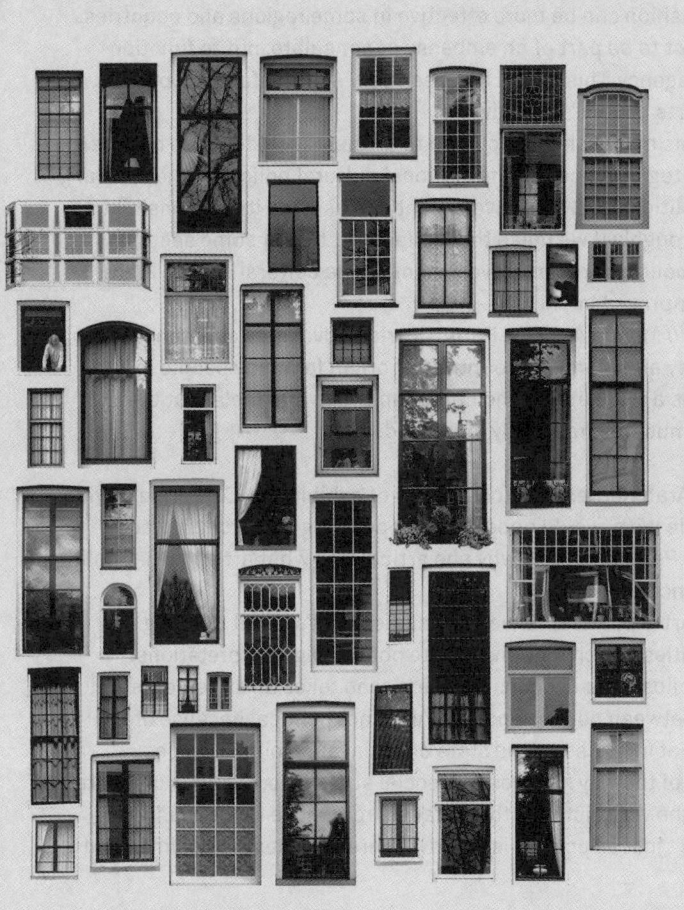

Windows are very big.
Are Dutch people open?

n between the ministries of Foreign Affairs (culture as lubrication
ations) and Cultural Affairs plus sundry public national founding
posts, as regards their role as cultural advocates. That difference of
en a fiction, in so far as it ever existed at all. All the same, operating
tal fashion can be more effective in some regions and countries.
n is not to be part of an embassy or consulate, but to function
art agency. This model has been very successfully adopted by,
iss 'arts council' Pro Helvetia.
ng this model should not lead to an increased distance between
d strategic choices in international cultural policy. On the contrary.
al/political level, the government can assume its responsibilities
d thoroughly if we make the implementation of some sections
ural policy more non-governmental. The cultural debate in the
be improved by this
itut du Monde Arabe in Paris, Dittrich advocates an intensification
Turkey and Morocco, countries of origin for many people in the
o sees a role here for the European Union and feels that the EU
and must be drastically increased.

rary Arab Representations' series of exhibitions, Catherine David,
itte de With, would appear to be operating at the cutting edge
itics. Perhaps that is why she articulates what art and what politics
a trenchant manner.
k of art is political as well as aesthetic. "It's about defining
ssibilities, which may give rise to conflicting interpretations."
ch philosopher Jacques Rancière, who takes an extremely subtle
hip between politics and art: "Art is not political because of the
gs that it carries on the state of social and political issues.
ause of the way it represents social structures, conflicts or identities.
e of the very distance that it takes from those functions."
litical, just as politics is an art. "There is an aesthetic dimension
s."

with this view that I would argue for a more intensive reciprocal
ts and politicians in the real world, each working from their own
ve more to offer each other than the relative mutual indifference

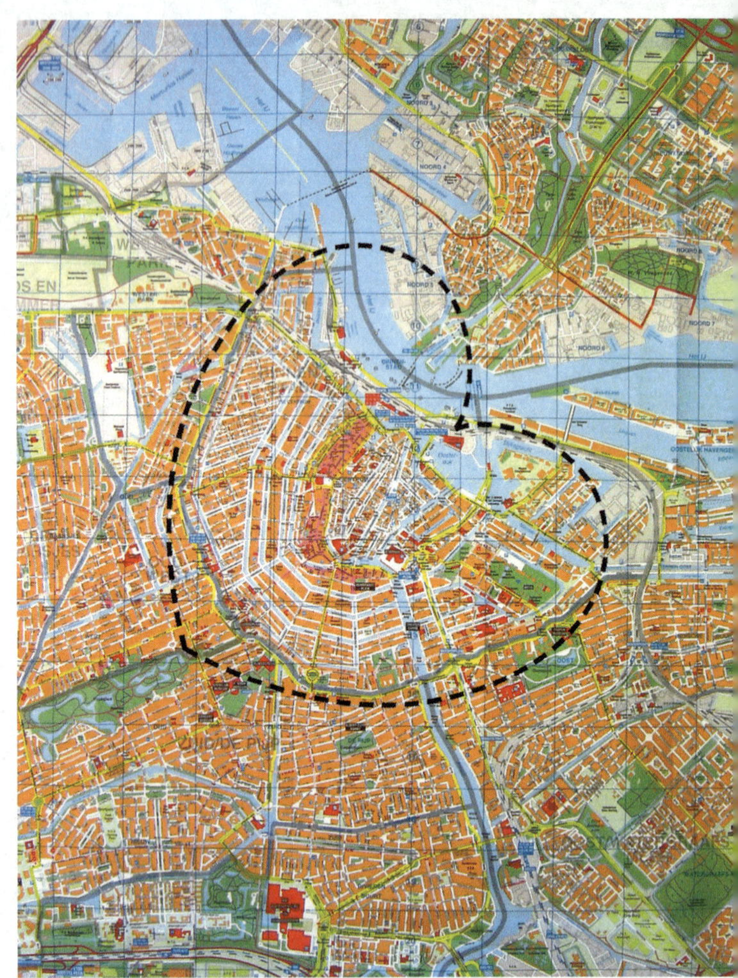

Dutch people are kind.

It may be because water(canal) makes people feel relaxed.

that exists between them at the moment in the Netherlands. A greater involvement
in society would be of benefit to both.
The essays on international cultural policy in this volume make one thing very clear:
not only are art and politics interdependent – they cannot exist without each other.

Ben Hurkmans has been director of the Fund for Amateur Art and the Performing Arts since 1998. Before that
he was director of the Theater School (at the Amsterdam School of the Arts) and the initiator and director
of the International Theater School Festival.

A Curator is Not a Politician
Catherine David interviewed by *Domeniek Ruyters*

In the last few years, Catherine David has worked intensively with Contemporary Arab Representations, which has in that period held exhibitions in Rotterdam, Barcelona and Umeå, and produced two multi-lingual (English/Spanish/Arabic) issues of the magazine *Tamàss*. An Iraqi platform will be inaugurated at Kunstwerk Berlin in December 2005 and developed further in Fundacio Tapies Barcelona. Contemporary Arab Representations in particular has earned Catherine David the reputation of being a politically interested curator, but from the following conversation it appears that this image requires a little adjustment.

You've always displayed a strong political interest as an exhibition maker. Is there a special reason for that?
—

A number of people claim that in three years in Rotterdam I only devoted attention to the Middle East, which is completely untrue. We exhibited a lot of other art, for example by Peter and Alison Smithson, young Mexican artists, Peter Friedl or Ulrike Ottinger. Furthermore, in response to your question I can tell you that every work of art, whether it's literature, cinema, music or visual art, is always a political and aesthetic articulation. It is about the definition of standpoints and possibilities, which perhaps gives rise to conflicting interpretations.
In order to avoid further misunderstanding and distance myself from certain simplifications I would like to quote French philosopher Jacques Ranciere: "Art is not political because of the messages and feelings that it carries on the state of social and political issues. It is not political because of the way it represents social structures, conflicts or identities. It is political by virtue of the very distance that it takes from those functions. It is political as it frames a specific space-time sensorium, as it redefines on this stage the power of speech or the co-ordinates of perception, shifts the places of the actor and spectator, etc. Because politics is not the exercise of power or the struggle for power. Politics is first of all the configuration of a space as political, the framing of a specific sphere of experience, the setting of objects posed as 'common' and subjects to whom the capacity is to recognize to designate these objects and to argue about them."[1] In order to make things clear and avoid again misunderstanding or the kind of systematic simplification which are polluting any attempt at serious thinking about the complex relationships between aesthetics and politics we should add: "In these terms there is an esthetical dimension immanent to politics. The suppression of this aesthetic is called consensus."[2]
I am afraid that the main obstacle to a real and serious debate on these issues in the Netherlands these days has to do with the development and imposition of a culture of consensus, not leaving much space for alternative analysis and voices.

So in practice there's no exhibition without political action?
—

It is honest to acknowledge that there is a relationship and not to suggest that making exhibitions is a neutral activity. At the same time, there are scores of ways of giving substance to that relationship. Take the art historian Serge Guilbaut, who in a study convincingly illustrated how the abstract-expressionist avantgarde in the United States has been used to found a world-wide American cultural empire. This policy continues to work through MoMa and can be seen as a striking example of cultural politics. On another level you can also consider that painter Robert Ryman is as political an artist as say Hans Haacke. He is just using a different critical paradigm; his deconstruction of the materiality of painting space is an astonishing critical gesture.

During Documenta X in 1997 you ostentatiously coupled politics with poesis. What was your intention there?
—

I guess to consider and show the complex articulations between politics and aesthetics developed in works from the late fifties on. And to give space to different perspectives and genealogies of what is called 'critical art'.

Is there really so much distance between these fields? Isn't there increasingly an overlap? Isn't the exhibition space more and more often a place where different forms of politics meet?
—

It is unavoidable within the complex circumstances Jacques Rancière is analysing above. In art you expect something to be opened up, something to be proposed, made possible; a new configuration of sensations and meanings.
It is very different from the practical solutions that many people, particularly politicians, are looking for. Artists aren't doctors. I think it's perverse and testifies to political opportunism if people expect art to offer a solution to a problem that politics has been consistently unable to solve.

It seems, however, that the political world has a different view, that it often uses art and culture with a political goal in mind. Culture is increasingly deployed as a political instrument, directed at a specific issue, such as the problem of the integration of Islamic cultures into Dutch society. Were you conscious of this dimension when you started with Contemporary Arab Representations?
—

From the beginning this project was willing to contribute to the consolidation of critical platforms developed, sometimes under very difficult conditions, in the region.
The challenge is to encourage production, circulation and exchange of projects by many different authors (visual artists, writers, architects and urbanists, intellectuals but also actors of social and political life) between the different centres of the Arab world on the one hand, and with the rest of the world on the other. That's also why the project was planned from the beginning as a long term one, including seminars, publications, travelling, performance and many other accompanying activities which could develop and make sense in context. After showing different aspects of the experimental and critical platform developed in Beirut in the last ten years, we focused on certain works produced in contemporary Cairo.
When the Beirut project was shown at Witte de With in Rotterdam people from the City Hall came to me asking why I didn't invite Moroccan or Turkish artists who would have been more representative of the city. This gives you an idea of the confusion we are in. Turks are not Arabs and of course there are more Moroccan than Lebanese

people in Rotterdam. But instead of pushing for the instrumentalisation of the project I would have found more productive that these same people try to understand why contemporary cultural production from Lebanon was so different from that of Moroccan people in Rotterdam. And I am afraid the reason why they are not able to think about that has to do with imposed communitarianism, paternalistic and patronising attitudes, and essentialisation of specific groups and culture.

The question for me in Rotterdam and the Netherlands is more how to change the relationship with the Moroccans than how to push Witte de With or any institution to do something 'special' to attract them. This could begin with the realization that most Moroccans came to the Netherlands in the 1960's for work, mainly from the Rif, from a poor countryside of traditional communities; that their integration is limited, their presence still thought of as 'temporary'. They hang around together, as though in exile here. Most of them share the experience of not belonging, and their cultural references are somehow more nostalgic than those that have developed in Morocco itself. They don't go to Witte de With to see contemporary Lebanese art and won't go unless many things change.

When seeing Contemporary Arab Representations it struck me that your interest in Arabic representation is not particularly Islamic in nature?
—

Here too we should avoid confusion. There is no Islamic art any more than there is Christian art these days. Except for specific works produced for church or mosque and religious practice. Strictly speaking the only contemporary Islamic art is maybe, as Agnès Devictor put it in an ironic way, Iranian cinema, as it is supposed to respect strict theological rules[3]. Furthermore I think it is important to remind people that Arab is not equivalent to Moslem; that Christians, Jews and other minorities have lived in the Arab world for a very long time; that Kabyles and Berbers are not Arab; and that many people from Moslem culture descent are not necessarily religious.

I would add that the Contemporary Arab Representations project began before September 11 and that I am convinced that the 'religious' explanation for the violent situation we are in now is a good way of denying the social, economical and political aspects of it. It is amazing to notice that since 2001 there have been no more political, economic and social problems, just 'terrorism'. Since instead of backing American state terrorism it would be safer and more decent to address the reasons for radicalisation. We should be serious and admit that what we see in Palestine or Iraq today has not much to do with Islam.

You work in a very person-oriented way, as a real curator, choosing for artistic quality. You select more for the person, as it were, than for representation. Do you plan the exhibitions deliberately as a corrective to the dominant forms of representation?
—

No, although I have to admit that after 11 September and the situation it created it's almost impossible to escape from polemical and resisting agenda. For me and under the circumstances I am working in at the moment collaboration with people is the primary thing and making possible and meaningful the artistic choice. Contemporary Arab Representations is growing into a concept with many layers, based on many contributions by people who usually operate from within various institutes. Together, the contributions have to articulate something of the complexity of the region and establish some distance from the simplistic and dominant idea that Arabic culture is essentially linked with calligraphy and colourful abstract art, and somehow produced out of the 'modern'. And also paying attention to the many dimensions and challenges of the esthetical experience, not just to the object. That's why we went for 'representations' (and not 'art') in the title, in order to emphasize the visual of course, but also textual and ideological representations.

Would you object if the exhibition became a factor in the political debate?
—

In the Netherlands positions are always drawn up so quickly. People always expect a simple solution, without debate and dissent. I don't believe this sort of attitude is getting us very far. It doesn't leave any space for the necessary 'suspension' of the ordinary co-ordinates of sensory experience and reframing of the overall network of relationships between spaces and times, subjects and objects, the common and the singular, which constitutes the esthetical experience.

In the accompanying publication to Contemporary Arab Representations, the magazine *Tamàss*, the Spanish professor Gema Martín Muñoz cited historian Samuel P. Huntington, who asserts that culture is increasingly becoming a form of politics and politics increasingly a form of culture. The 'clash of civilisations' is used in defence of the war in Iraq, but Muñoz seeks the cause elsewhere, not in cultural difference. She sees it as a political conflict.
—

What Muñoz is severely deconstructing is the essentialization of culture Huntington works with. This is a very old and cheap idea, and he probably never understood 'Orientalism' by Edward Saïd. So Muñoz is making clear that there's no essential and static Arabic culture, defined once and for all, without movement and change, just as there is no static European culture either. The most challenging aspect of Contemporary Arab Representations could be the contribution to the complexity of the images, to de-essentializing it and to giving more visibility to ideas and forms which have nothing to do with Huntington propaganda.

How as a curator do you prevent yourself being transformed into an instrument of the ruling politics?
—

Speaking honestly and seeing how things are going at the moment, I can't imagine that a small programme like Contemporary Arab Representations could introduce the very complicated Arabic and Islamic cultures in any way that would be of use to a government. It also seems that a minimum of radicalism and coherence in your work is the best antidote to political instrumentalization.

Would you find it objectionable to be included in a larger information project by the government? Concerning Islamic issues, for example, or European identity.
—

Why not? But surely not under the label of 'Islamic' issues which I find extremely suspect. And if this were the case I would insist on collaborating with an institute like ISIM, the Institute for the Study of Islam in the Modern World located in Leiden, which studies Islamic cultures world-wide. In Rotterdam, I was always amazed that this expert centre was totally ignored. But more importantly I don't understand why our project in particular should be used for this sort of objective. Ultimately, it all comes down to stimulating interest, and that can't be imposed from the outside. From an early age I was raised with respect for and interest in Arabic culture and I get closer through friends at school and travelling. I don't know how I could cultivate that sort of interest in people just through an exhibition when there is only indifference or ignorance around. It can only happen if interest is present to some degree beforehand. There should be a minimum desire and empathy.

Do you think that art can contribute to improving the situation in the Netherlands?
—

That's difficult to say. As long as you are using words as 'allogenous people'.
I have my doubts.

Does France do things better when it comes to these sorts of issues around integration and the internationalisation of the culture?
—

France could and should do much better due to its colonial (and anti-colonial) history, as well as a tradition of immigration. A lot of time has been lost during the last fifteen to twenty years due to lack of political intelligence and courage, due to the weakening of the republican pact, and a lot of confusion was created on purpose around immigration issues. A long discussion would have been necessary.
There is no doubt that despite the racism and aggressive feelings you can observe in many places, there are also many examples of empathy, of enjoying a cosmopolitan city, of experimenting with complex proximities I see more in Paris than in other places.

Does that mean that the Netherlands has a structural problem, which we can't do very much about?
—

Of course something can be done about it. And a lot is already being done. Look at the Rotterdam International Film Festival with its programming of non-western films. It's important to confront people with the mechanisms that have crept in surreptitiously. A word like *allochtoon* (non-western migrant) is an awful term, authoritarian and discriminating. The Netherlands is supposed to have a liberal tradition but at the moment everything is very much "don't touch me and I won't touch you". So small minded. Everything's mired in the polder. In the Netherlands these days, I always have the acute feeling of being at the end station of the continent of Europe. Even in London, which is not particularly my favourite city, I experience more of a European dynamic. And the Netherlands is so focused on America and neo-liberal values too, more so than any other country in Europe. It's so materialistic and lacking in speculative energy.

Domeniek Ruyters is editor-in-chief of *Metropolis M*, a bimonthly magazine on contemporary art. He publishes articles in Dutch and international magazines and catalogues and is an art critic for *de Volkskrant.*

1 - in *Malaise dans l'esthétique*, Galilée, 2004

2 - idem

3 - in *Politique du cinéma Iranien*, CNRS, 2005

On the Wrong Foot: Branding and Identity Promotion in International Cultural Relations

Divergent perspectives
—

Cultural policy is an eminently European invention, developed intensively over the last sixty years by practically all governments on the Continent. It is based on a widespread conviction that the development of extensive cultural infrastructure and access to it by all parts of the population is a public interest, benefiting society and assuring its general wellbeing. This noble conviction, however, has been contaminated over the years by the ideological predilections and rivalries of the Cold War era and, more recently, has suffered from the onslaught of the neo-liberal ideology of glorifying the market and its magic fix. It has been further eroded by the striving of many governments to reduce expenditures and to distance themselves from some traditional public spheres of engagement. All this fashionable talk about public-private partnership, for example, reflects their desire to see some of the burden shifted to the private sector, although under as yet unspecified conditions. The very notion of culture has also been altered by the explosive growth of the cultural industry (design, fashion, certain types of music, film, publishing) alongside the traditional institutional matrix of arts, cultural heritage, libraries etc. In addition, governments have begun developing more specific expectations of their investment in culture: as a contribution to social cohesion, as a stimulus to tourism and the culture industry, to job creation, crime reduction and competitiveness. Nonetheless, when it comes to international cultural co-operation, most European governments continue to see this sort of engagement as their primary responsibility, as an aspect of traditional foreign policy within the proper domains of government

Politicians and government officials traditionally think of international cultural co-operation in bilateral terms because during the long Cold War period it was instigated, financed, directed and often directly managed by governments and their specialised agencies as a matter of public diplomacy and overall influence enhancement abroad. In the post-Cold War period, however, international cultural co-operation has become increasingly multilateral, with complex collaborative forms evolving far beyond simple bilateral exchange, increasingly driven by the growing initiatives and autonomy of the cultural operators themselves. From their point of view, the role of governments should be to provide funds for collaborative cross-border ventures and not to meddle, arbitrate, steer or seek to co-ordinate what the operators choose to do.

For politicians and governments, this emancipation of the cultural field is not so self-evident and the acceptance of the limited role of subsidy does not come easily. Funding means allocating public money and that implies a policy, which in turn means clear procedures, priorities within the available budget, selection criteria and an analysis of the effects of expenditures made. But in defining objectives, criteria and procedures, civil servants and their political bosses still tend to see international cultural co-operation primarily as a way of exporting national prestige and improving the image of the nation and government abroad. Influenced by the pep talks of marketing experts, some civil servants even talk nowadays about their own country as a brand and perceive international cultural co-operation as a means of making the brand flashier. Alternatively, they rationalise their support in economic terms, as an initial export stimulus that will in due course bring further gains to the national tourist industry or to the cultural sector.

While such expectations may be legitimate under European Union regulations and World Trade Organization rules, they are often far-fetched and certainly inapplicable to the majority of international projects in the performing and visual arts. Most cultural operators are not driven by brand considerations and tend to see themselves as unique players and not as part of the tourism or culture industries. Most of them are indifferent to their government's political and geo-strategic considerations. Rather than being influenced by the prospects of fame and fortune, they are motivated by the interests of their own art and artistic development, by eccentric curiosity and a desire to experiment.

These divergent approaches by governmental subsidy distributors on the one hand and operators seeking government support on the other set the stage for perpetual misunderstandings, mutual blame and shared disappointments.

Promotion instead of co-operation
—

If voters demand good governance with transparency and accountability and expect government support of selected public domains to have concrete objectives and results, this should apply to international cultural co-operation as well. One would hope to see these objectives clearly formulated in public documents of a strategic nature - that is, for the longer term - and developed in dialogue with the cultural operators prior to receiving the appropriate democratic endorsement, including parliamentary support. This rarely happens in European countries. Objectives are usually framed, if at all, in general terms of promotion of peace and international understanding, and international appreciation of a country's own culture and tradition, while the decision-making process has a more pragmatic course guided by current circumstances and opportunism. Policy statements are sparse, copied from old papers and reiterating outdated rhetoric, and they lack an analytical basis or a fresh battery of arguments and ideas for implementation. Especially in the newly independent countries of Central and Eastern Europe, statements of objectives are larded with nation-building urgencies and an identity-centred preoccupation with the national culture that is perceived as a precious commodity deserving of much more status abroad than it currently has. Some countries hastily set up their own machinery for promoting national culture, or increase the number of their cultural centres in other countries - without ever questioning their efficiency. Days, weeks, months and entire seasons spent promoting the film, ceramics, music, fashion or literature of country X in country Y are ever more frequent in Western Europe. France and the UK seem to be the primary targets.

Even in countries that could reasonably be expected to act with less cultural insecurity given their history, size, political influence and economic weight, the promotional motive seems to prevail. If there is a public discussion at all, the worried guardians of national identity, made nervous by globalisation, European integration and especially the demographic changes caused by migration, appear as boosters and promoters of the national culture and dominate the field over the cultural operators who see

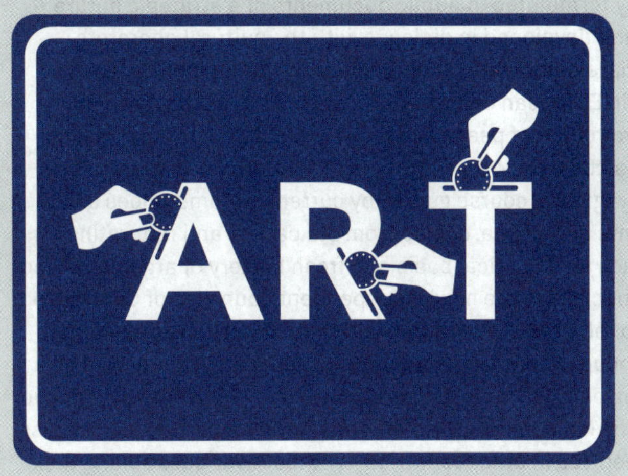

he government invests in ART.

utch creators are lucky.

istic development, by eccentric curiosity and a desire to experiment.

roaches by governmental subsidy distributors on the one hand
ng government support on the other set the stage for perpetual
mutual blame and shared disappointments.

f co-operation

od governance with transparency and accountability and expect
of selected public domains to have concrete objectives and
apply to international cultural co-operation as well. One would hope
ves clearly formulated in public documents of a strategic nature -
r term - and developed in dialogue with the cultural operators
e appropriate democratic endorsement, including parliamentary
happens in European countries. Objectives are usually framed,
rms of promotion of peace and international understanding, and
iation of a country's own culture and tradition, while the decision-
a more pragmatic course guided by current circumstances and
statements are sparse, copied from old papers and reiterating
nd they lack an analytical basis or a fresh battery of arguments and
ation. Especially in the newly independent countries of Central and
ements of objectives are larded with nation-building urgencies
red preoccupation with the national culture that is perceived as a
deserving of much more status abroad than it currently has. Some
up their own machinery for promoting national culture, or increase
cultural centres in other countries - without ever questioning their
ks, months and entire seasons spent promoting the film, ceramics,
erature of country X in country Y are ever more frequent in Western
the UK seem to be the primary targets.

at could reasonably be expected to act with less cultural insecurity
ize, political influence and economic weight, the promotional
vail. If there is a public discussion at all, the worried guardians of
de nervous by globalisation, European integration and especially
anges caused by migration, appear as boosters and promoters
re and dominate the field over the cultural operators who see

and newspaper columnist Theo van Gogh? Might the real values of th
cultural constellation not be better shared within an emerging Euro
in a less directive and more spontaneous manner?

One cannot help noticing the alarming growth of international confe
cultural identity, organized or sponsored by governments and their s
agencies as another clear indication that European governments rer
narrow promotional interests. These interests are motivated in turn
subconscious anxieties about eroding monolithic concepts of natior
national culture, even when such anxieties are masked by fashionab
inter-cultural dialogue and cultural diversity.

Transparency of criteria and procedures is another issue. Cultural o
complain that it is difficult in Europe to figure out when, where and f
government will be willing to give its support. The artistic value and
specific project often remain in the shadow of political and geo-strat
Projects depend on special moments (a forthcoming state visit, a rot
an anniversary of diplomatic relations) or are conditioned by specific
(visibility, emblematic nature, added value) that have nothing to do v
and dynamics of cultural production. International cultural co-opera
code for engagements that are clearly of a manifestational and repr
Artists, on the other hand, often contemplate projects that envisage
experimentation and creation, and do not necessarily result in an imn
for large audiences. Representational anxiety apparently motivates
French quango Association Française d'Action Artistique, hiding beh
status of a citizens' association (*loi* 1901), to maintain unofficial lists
worthy of representing the French *gloire* abroad with the support of
How these lists are composed and updated has for years been a sub
guessing among French cultural operators and their European colle

A steady tension
—

For the cultural operators it would make sense to strive to gain a bett
the concerns and sensitivities of politicians and civil servants when it
of international cultural co-operation. The more aware cultural opera
whelming concerns of those who allocate government subsidies, the

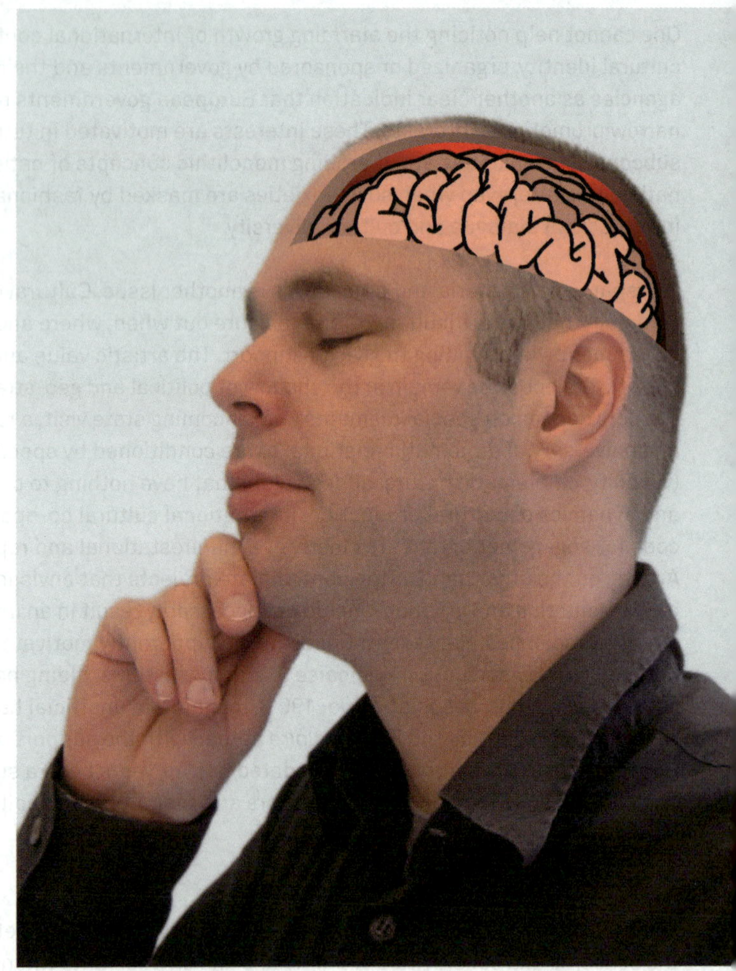

The beauty of Dutch is
clients considers about the culture.

their international work chiefly in a developmental perspective. Whereas the Goethe Institute might describe its work abroad as a dialogue between cultures and not as plugging German culture, the Bundestag remains watchful from a promotional corner, ever ready to criticise and complain about *Nestbeschimpfung*. The Dutch parliament was enthusiastic about the government's intention to set up a Dutch cultural centre in Brussels, whereas neither the Dutch nor the Belgian cultural operators felt a need for such a facility. And recently, arguing for the assertive promotion of 'Dutchness' at home and abroad in terms of national cultural and historical identity, commentator Paul Scheffer has called for government-sponsored Dutch cultural institutes to be set up in all the new member states of the EU. The question is: can such one-sided institutional solutions hide the cracks in the façade of Dutch tolerance, exposed by the burning of churches, mosques and schools in the wake of the killing of filmmaker and newspaper columnist Theo van Gogh? Might the real values of the current Dutch cultural constellation not be better shared within an emerging European cultural space, in a less directive and more spontaneous manner?

One cannot help noticing the alarming growth of international conferences on national cultural identity, organized or sponsored by governments and their specialised agencies as another clear indication that European governments remain driven by narrow promotional interests. These interests are motivated in turn by diffuse, almost subconscious anxieties about eroding monolithic concepts of nation, identity, and national culture, even when such anxieties are masked by fashionable phrases like inter-cultural dialogue and cultural diversity.

Transparency of criteria and procedures is another issue. Cultural operators often complain that it is difficult in Europe to figure out when, where and for what a government will be willing to give its support. The artistic value and viability of a specific project often remain in the shadow of political and geo-strategic considerations. Projects depend on special moments (a forthcoming state visit, a rotating EU presidency, an anniversary of diplomatic relations) or are conditioned by specific requirements (visibility, emblematic nature, added value) that have nothing to do with the temporality and dynamics of cultural production. International cultural co-operation becomes a code for engagements that are clearly of a manifestational and representational nature. Artists, on the other hand, often contemplate projects that envisage joint learning, experimentation and creation, and do not necessarily result in an immediate presentation for large audiences. Representational anxiety apparently motivates the specialised French quango Association Française d'Action Artistique, hiding behind the nominal status of a citizens' association (*loi* 1901), to maintain unofficial lists of artists deemed worthy of representing the French *gloire* abroad with the support of taxpayers' money. How these lists are composed and updated has for years been a subject of much wild guessing among French cultural operators and their European colleagues.

A steady tension

—

For the cultural operators it would make sense to strive to gain a better understanding of the concerns and sensitivities of politicians and civil servants when it comes to matters of international cultural co-operation. The more aware cultural operators are of the over-whelming concerns of those who allocate government subsidies, the better equipped they should become to offer their own arguments, to counter implausible expectations and to point out the contradictions between the fatalistic belief in globalisation and markets on the one hand and knee-jerk state interventionism on the other. It is easy to guess that most cultural operators would be only too quick to raise concerns about the autonomy of their work. But autonomy is a notion that needs to be reconsidered and redefined again and again, in relation to public authorities, market forces and private foundations, audiences and other cultural operators. It must not become a worn-out, automatically invoked mantra. If cultural operators expect public support for some of their international co-operative ventures, they had better be aware of the existing political priorities and considerations. Only then can they maximise the support they need fully to realise their artistic intentions within the political margins this support imposes.

Even better, they can contrast their own political impulses, interests and priorities with those articulated by governmental institutions. One could expect artists who seek to engage in a complicated artistic venture in the western Balkans, Turkey or occupied Palestine, for instance, to integrate their artistic aspirations with their own political analyses and sense of political priorities, to view their own artistic resources as political capital to be invested in a particular spot with the expectation of political results. In the Dutch landscape, invocations of artistic autonomy in relation to the political considerations of government are still more frequent than invocations of an artist's own political goals as an alternative to those promulgated by government and implicated in funding decisions. This is not a nostalgic call for a return to the old-fashioned and romantic notion of engagement but rather a criticism of artistic narcissism, masked as autonomy, which refuses to articulate its own conception of global citizenship. What is needed is artistic and political involvement in the furthering of global justice and equality, in opposing discriminatory, exclusionary and exploratory politics. It is the dialectic of political and artistic, financial and creative, governmental and civic differences that in each instance needs to be rephrased, re-examined and resolved.

Politicians and civil servants need to grasp the shifting meaning of contemporary culture as well. It is not just a sector, encompassing our cultural heritage, the arts and culture industry, but a transversal dimension of social and individual life, invoking expression, freedom, creativity, values, lifestyles, social cohesion and intercultural competence. The role of politics is to offer, stimulate, and encourage – not to proscribe, limit and impose. It should be driven by an awareness of the cultural consequences of economic globalisation (growing uniformity of cultural products, imposed by the oligopolies) and by an understanding of Europe as a community of citizens and as an integrated zone of creativity and rich cultural diversity, not by obsessions or anxieties about identity, derived from an anachronistic cultural nationalism. Such exclusionary and rejectionist stances of nations and national cultural systems carry a plausible danger (as Dutch historian and writer Geert Mak points out in a recent booklet *Gedoemd tot kwetsbaarheid* 2005) of truncated traditions and a self-imposed insularity and provincialism. Whether the government gives prominence to social cohesion or competitiveness, to social benefits or economic gain in supporting culture, it is dealing with creative energies, engaging in the governance of creativity (even in matters of cultural heritage, its protection and validation). This is a vulnerable field that thrives on opportunities and risk-taking, courageous investment, openness and flexibility. Public support for international cultural co-operation creates a climate in which cultural operators can peek across borders to observe and seek out partners in collaborative ventures for the sake of their own development and stimulation. It also encourages a climate of hospitality and generosity in which foreign cultural operators will be invited to visit, stimulating and focusing their curiosity. Both aspects ultimately benefit audiences – both at home and abroad – by making them more discriminating and demanding. It is an investment in European citizenship, as opposed to nation-building. To reduce a rich, dynamic cultural constellation in one country to a brand, and then to judge cultural cross-border activities in terms of their potential brand enhancement, is no way to do justice to the creative energies of even a single medium-sized city.

One cannot expect Dutch successes in dance, film, design, fashion, literature, music and performing arts or the Netherlands' leading museums and exquisite historic monuments to offset the negative publicity that Dutch drug policy, euthanasia, homosexual marriages and political murders have apparently created in some places abroad. The news that many Dutch families are considering emigration due to the current turmoil makes the front pages of the European press (*International Herald Tribune*, 28 February 2005) while the excellence of a Nederlands Dans Theater premiere will have limited international coverage, tucked away on the arts pages. Johann Simons' successes on the German stage won't reduce the exposure of controversial MP Hirsi Ali on German TV. However, the achievements of Dutch architecture, design and, more recently, fashion do shape positive expectations of other architects, designers and couturiers coming from the Netherlands, occasionally giving them a competitive edge in attracting international attention.

Two hypotheses
—
While the traces of the Cold War may be disappearing rather quickly, the ultimate test of a democratic government still is how to engage in the stimulation of cultural prosperity at home and abroad without sliding into political propaganda, jingoistic parades and trivial commercialism. The much discussed terrorist threat - plausible but invisible, ubiquitous but evasive, international in both its recruitment practices and its selection of targets - makes culture today an important security issue. A sense of cultural security won't be created by efforts to score points abroad as a state, nation or government or by the imposition of cultural boundaries, reinforced by extra locks, but by an attitude to be nurtured by increased cultural mobility and international co-operation, put into daily practice by most cultural operators, not just the most successful and prestigious. Ultimately, this attitude has to be translated into the enthusiasm of audiences, measured by their receptiveness to cultural products that at first glance may seem strange, foreign, or unfamiliar but that appeal to them and sway their options not because they are Dutch or Estonian but because they have the capacity to stir the imagination.

Misunderstandings and tensions between cultural operators seeking support for international cultural co-operation and the political and civil service apparatus that can give or withdraw that support will likely continue. Even if more artists develop nomadic career patterns, the institutions that produce and present their work will probably remain anchored in their national cultural systems and largely dependent on their support. Hence, instead of a conclusion, two cautious hypotheses for the future:

First, the more EU integration advances and the more Europe emerges as an inclusive dynamic and divergent cultural space, the more likely public authorities are to reduce their promotional efforts in supporting international cultural co-operation, freeing themselves from their preoccupation with the nation state and its culture. But at the same time, the debate about the cultural image Europe presents to the rest of the world and the capacity of cultural products to enhance and affirm (that is: to represent and promote) that image will intensify.

Second, if the European Constitution is rejected in some of the national referenda to be held in ten EU member states in 2005 and 2006, the process of European integration will lose much of its impetus and enter into a protracted period of malaise and doubt. The EU will scale back to chiefly an economic arrangement, sustained at a minimum of mutual convenience, and the common approach to political and security issues will be shelved and cultural policy re-nationalised. As a result, public support for international cultural co-operation will be weighed down by even more promotional and representational objectives. Cultural operators will continue to resent this instrumentalisation, accept public support with a mixture of opportunism and complaint, and seek to offset political expectations with appealing market-driven alternatives – if not in London, Paris, Amsterdam or Milan, then perhaps in Johannesburg, Moscow, Rio and Shanghai.

Dragan Klaic is a theatre scholar, cultural analyst and author. Formerly the director of the Theater Instituut Nederland, he now is affiliated with the Felix Meritus, *European Centre for Arts and Sciences* and with the University of Leiden as a scholar and teacher of art and cultural policy. His most recent publication is *Europe as a Cultural Project* (2005).

Politics and Culture are Hard to Separate
Els van der Plas interviewed by *Sandra Jongenelen*

International Dutch cultural policy is, in a number of ways, pure politics, says Els van der Plas, Director of the Prince Claus Fund. "Dutch involvement in a cultural project in Surinam harks back to the time of our colonial rule, and has little to do with the quality of the art or arts involved."

Van der Plas finds this unjustifiable. "The point of departure should always be cultural quality and we shouldn't allow ourselves to be driven by politics or historical links. A country of cultural interest may be of no political interest to Holland whatever. That's a shame, but it shouldn't stop us."

Burkina Faso is just such an example. For twenty years the film and television festival Fespace has been held in that West African country, but now for the first time the most recent festival, at the beginning of March 2005, was discussed in papers such as *El Pais*, *Le Monde* and the *NRC Handelsblad,* which may have something to do with the international recognition African film has recently received.

In February, South African Marc Dornford-May won the Golden Bear for best film, with *U-Carmen e-Khayelitsha* at the Berlin Film Festival. At the San Sebastian Festival, screenwriter Fanta Nacro from Burkina Faso won the Montblanc Award for the script for *La Nuit de la Vérité*. And South African Darrell Roodt's *Yesterday* was nominated for an Oscar.

"If Africa is in the spotlight of the film world, the Dutch should be paying attention," says Van der Plas. "And we should be going to Bamako in Mali to see the photography. I say this at gatherings with representatives from the Ministry of Foreign Affairs." In practice things haven't progressed that far, but Van der Plas does notice a change in artists' attitudes. "It used to be that no one wanted to go to Hanoi, only to New York. That's no longer the case."

On the face of it, it would seem obvious that international cultural policy would have strong links with the political legacy. Political interests always play a role in cultural policy. "In countries where we're active, culture and politics are hard to separate", emphasizes the Fund Director. "The simple fact of being an artist in some countries is already a political statement. If you are involved in making art, it's always about something. Moreover, being an artist often ensures a less-than-attractive economic position."

In the Netherlands too, it is an illusion to think that culture and politics can be separated. "In spite of the liberal politician Thorbecke, who felt that art is no concern of the government, our culture is steered by politics. The system of subsidies is not without value-judgements. Our political choices are the result of our cultural characteristics. Look at Prime Minister Balkenende and you'll see our Christian traditions." What applies to photography in Mali (Bamako) and film in Burkina Faso (Ouagadougou) also applies to the arts market in China. "What's being made there at the moment is much more interesting than what's happening in Holland", said Sebastian Lopez recently. He is the Co-Curator of the Shanghai Biennial and Director of the Gate Foundation Amsterdam, an institute for contemporary non-Western visual arts.

Van der Plas agrees. "If you want to get ahead, you have to go to Beijing. China is both culturally and economically intriguing and must inevitably be an important political factor in the future. We look far too much to New York and Berlin. China will become a fascinating cultural market. Just watch: soon the Chinese will be buying Rineke Dijkstra's photographs."

A public with traditional taste has already found its way to the West; buyers of Chinese and Japanese porcelain at Sotheby's auction in Amsterdam are generally around seventy per cent non-Westerners, according to figures produced by expert Feng-Chun Ma a number of years ago. At first the buyers were mostly Europeans, Americans and Hong Kong Chinese, but for the last six years, private individuals and dealers from China have been increasingly visible. "There are more and more extremely wealthy Chinese prepared to pay very high prices," says Ma from her own experience. "That's a development that people here in the Netherlands are not yet aware of."

For the Prince Claus Fund, the cultural and economic explosion is reason enough to organize a China trip with the Mondriaan Foundation, the Princessenhof from Leeuwarden, and some others. 'In May, we'll show the curators and critics what's going on in China. We hope it will stimulate them to plan an exhibition."

These two trusts, along with Artists' Initiative W139 went to the Middle East. "As a result, the Director of the Kunsthal, Wim Pijbes, is toying with the idea of putting together an exhibition of work by an Iranian photographer from before the ayatollahs," says Van der Plas.

To mark the seventieth birthday of the consort to Queen Beatrix, The Prince Claus Fund was set up in 1996, with the aim of supporting activities in the fields of culture and development. It awards prizes, brings out publications and organises exchange programmes with artists in Africa, Asia, the Middle East, Latin America and the Caribbean. The annual budget of almost four million euros comes from the Ministry of Foreign Affairs and the National Postcode Lottery.

The people or organizations with whom the Prince Claus Fund co-operates are generally socially engaged artists, academics, writers and thinkers from 'difficult' countries: Angola, Afghanistan, Rwanda, Mozambique, Cambodia. Critics sometimes ask: "Do you have to support a poetry festival in Medellin? Wouldn't it be better instead to do something about the drugs problem in Colombia?" Van der Plas replies: "People need to take pride in their surroundings, be given something positive. That is hugely underestimated. Culture is a basic need, just like a home and food. Culture gives people validation, respect and identity. It says something about their origins. That's why blowing up the Buddhas in Afghanistan was so tragic, as was the plundering of the National Museum in Baghdad."

Supporting oppressed artists serves another cause. "Artists are often the conscience of a country. In many African countries, they have more influence than here. But in the Netherlands too, their importance should not be underestimated. Ali B. gives people another image of Moroccans, as did the record attendance at the recent Morocco exhibition in Amsterdam, which was shown for four months (from 17 December 2004 to 17 April 2005) in the Nieuwe Kerk."

The Prince Claus Fund is first and foremost a cultural organization, but it does not avoid politics. On the contrary, every decision requires constant navigation between culture and politics. "We once described ourselves as Amnesty for culture," explains the director of the Fund.

Van der Plas has been involved with the Fund from the outset. After studying art history in Utrecht, she worked at the Rijksmuseum voor Volkenkunde (Ethnology) in Leiden, after which she set up the Gate Foundation where she served for ten years, before moving on to take over the helm of the Prince Claus Fund.

The political side of her work has much to do with the situation in the countries where the Fund is active. "If a dictator takes over, you have to make some careful choices. We will not support anyone who works for a dictatorial regime. They probably won't produce good art anyway, although who knows?"

Quality is the most important criterion at the Prince Claus Fund, but the pros and cons of awarding a prize remain tricky. "Do you choose a poet who writes wonderfully or someone who writes a little less wonderfully, but who is an example in the face of the opposition? If he or she is a bad poet, it's easy: no. But in the case of a reasonably good poet? Then you really have to think hard before deciding."

The Fund often tries to communicate a political message via a personal story. "Say, after a long search during the war in the Congo, you find someone who's a practising artist. You can decide to support them in order to attract attention to the cultural situation in that country. There is a requirement that the artist's work be of a certain quality. That is separate from politics and can be objectively appraised. If we're not sure, we refuse. The best choice is for quality, then no one will be compromised."

A glance at past winners of the Prince Claus Awards clearly demonstrates the combination of quality and social engagement. The main prize of one hundred thousand euros was awarded last year to Mahmoud Darwish (Palestine), one of the most famous poets in the Arabic world, who has been living in exile for more than twenty-six years. A prize of twenty-five thousand euros was awarded to Jawad Al Assadi (Iraq), an innovative theatre-maker who fled into exile from Saddam Hussein's dictatorship and lived in various Arabic countries for twenty-five years.

Poet Tin Moe (Union of Myanmar, formerly Burma) is another example. Before the military dictatorship his work was known and appreciated everywhere. Since the takeover, and his imprisonment, he lives in exile in Belgium and the United States but informally he is Burma's national poet laureate. He has been writing for over half a century. Even the generals who imprisoned him in 1991 learned to read from his schoolbooks. Van der Plas: "Tin Moe received the prize because he is a good poet, but also in order to draw attention to Burma."

Van der Plas is wary of using culture purely as a means to an end. "Cultural exchange is interesting with every country. But should you use it for something you can't solve politically? It can offer an opening. That is possible. Culture leads to better understanding. When Dutch people go to a performance of Turkish singers, they realize what an enormous wealth that culture has to offer. The same applies to the archeological sites in the Middle East. They are a thousand times more impressive than anything we have. People should see the sites in Turkey or Jordan. It helps mutual cultural-historical understanding. Intercultural dialogue is always a good thing, though you can't expect it to change the world. It's a matter of small steps."

Sandra Jongenelen is a freelance journalist for *Het Financieele Dagblad* and *Kunstbeeld*, and a member of the advisory council for *Boekman*, a journal for art, culture and policy.

Art as a Permanent Hint

Culture is back on the political agenda. After decades of being relegated to the ghetto of the subsidy circuit and the sponsored outings of the more chic institutions, art appears to have broken out of its restricted domain. Politicians are suddenly making a fuss about art. Their attitude says much about how far apart art and politics have grown over the years: the new interest is driven by a concern for public order – or actually, pure fear. The paradox of the situation, apart from the fact that art was unable to find its way out of its isolation by itself, is that art has now become politicised by public reaction to a work of art that does not immediately appeal to the imagination *as a work of art*. What's more, the fact that the film *Submission* by Ayaan Hirsi Ali and the recently murdered Theo van Gogh leaves so little to the imagination (and thus ignores the art world's accepted criteria of assessment) is very likely a necessary condition for the transition to another domain: the street and politics.

A new relationship between art and politics is now evolving – strangely enough, because a politically driven work of art was experienced not as a political but religious insult. This has put pressure on all sorts of neat dividing lines typical of secular post-modern society. How is the triangle of politics-religion-art to be realigned now? And who ever would have thought that we would be posing these questions only five years into a new century?

In order to begin answering them, we must look at what has come to an end. European art of the 20th century is characterised by tremendous autonomous development that was not driven by political or religious systems. Art became a separate domain, with its own language, rules, dynamics, and assessment criteria. This is what modernism is about. The well-known paradox is that art pays for its freedom: in order to be able to evolve within its own domain, that domain is simultaneously, and necessarily, 'lured away' from other domains. This holds true for the artistic domain as a whole and also for the various artistic sub-domains.
In the artistic domain, the reigning axiom is 'art without utilitarian value', because the concept of utility had been perverted by political and/or economic interests. A shift also took place within the classic duality of the 'Morally Good' and the 'Beautiful' – in favour of the beautiful, which started to write and then dictate its own rules. This led to the final stage, in which art removed itself from politics, and politics definitively placed art in a ghetto.
When we consider this development, not only in the aftermath of a horrible crime, but also from the broader perspective of a new relationship between culture and politics, we must ask ourselves whether a new balance can be found between the morally good and the beautiful. In place of beauty defined by criteria developed entirely within the domain of the Arts as it today, what we might be searching for is a movement out of this domain, into the social/cultural/ethical domain of the morally good. This can be seen as a social challenge. But in which area (in the broadest sense of the word: geographical, political, psychological, cultural-philosophical) could this development occur, and how could we prevent it from simply degenerating into pure regression? For that is the

greatest danger: silencing art in the interest of public order can very easily lead to the elimination of everything controversial. And in the past decades we have had enough of 'socially involved art', a trend that led to monsters who had nothing to do with art and found no target group for their social involvement.

In any case, terms such as 'area' and 'domain' make it clear that a space is at stake. Culture will have to be given space in order to be taken seriously again. Only then, as the German Islamist Bassam Tibi says, can a multicultural Europe offer its citizens a foothold. In a recent address at the conference 'Europe: A beautiful Idea?' organized by the Nexus Institute, Tibi maintained that Europe is incapable of forming a successful integration policy because it holds itself in disdain. As a concept, 'Europe' does not offer enough scope for self-identification. According to Tibi, European identity should rest on the quality of its cultural exchange – it is this quality which differentiates Europe from other continents, where mutual recognition sooner takes place within the domains of religion or the market. In a sense, Tibi is arguing for a re-evaluation, a vitalisation, of public space.
Perhaps it is time to take Tibi's analysis into consideration, for it seems to fit in with a reorientation that is taking place at all sorts of levels. The current discussion on standards of decency and behaviour is one example. And anyone who speaks with young architects from Eastern Europe, as I recently did for a documentary project, will notice that their history makes them very sympathetic toward the idea of a moral function for public space. They are surprised and concerned about the ease with which that space is ceded to Wild West capitalists.

The recommendations made by Bassam Tibi and the architects with whom I spoke are radical: they require an extensive restructuring of existing 'spaces'. This means, for instance, that the mass media must be stimulated to offer culture (*'Art Because It's a Must'* is the cynical title of a television programme that considers itself trapped in a fixed structure of programming. That title ought to be taken dead seriously!).
It also means that art should be given a matter-of-course place in public space: on the streets, the squares, in buildings, at bus stops, in the metro – art as a constant hint at other ways of being. In this space, a new language could arise that no longer defines the Other in terms that are economic ('the guest worker'), ethnic ('the Turk'), or religious ('the Muslim'), but accepts everyone within the shared cultural space (or spiritual space – a word that Tibi and the Eastern European architects have no problem with at all). This could include political-cultural initiatives that open up sections of public space and public utilitarian facilities to projects not determined by efficiency or market mechanisms. For example, anyone observing the giant ads for phone sex posted along route A4 between Amsterdam and The Hague can experience a whole gamut of thoughts and emotions: you could call them in bad taste or a contamination of public space. That is a secular standpoint. From certain political or cultural perspectives, you could also say that they are repressive, insulting or offensive. The question here is whether the market should have the last word on the furbishing of public space, or if the government has a social responsibility in this regard. Like the 'Marlboro man' billboards along that same route, which disappeared because they were contrary to public health policy, all sorts of advertisements could be declared at variance with a cultural ideal. In their stead could come a continual variety of artworks along the motorways, in trains, buses, trams, metros and waiting areas; in short, all of the places we share,

and where we will no longer put up with being confronted by nothing but the language of commerce, which alienates us from other values. In these places we can write a story together; or actually, write all of our stories, side-by-side. Something like this could be a European project. Few people are so open to impressions as fourteen-to-sixteen-year-olds when they travel. Put them in a train that popularises Goethe.

Such an endeavour implies that the notion of 'quality' should be on the political agenda whenever decisions affecting citizens' daily lives are made. This could occasionally be at odds with efficiency, which has been elevated to the highest norm by the managers who call themselves politicians nowadays. In its stead must come a democratising movement that dares to mobilise culture (and not the market, the nation or even values) as the lowest common denominator, and experiment with the synchronicity and equality of different 'stories', all of which deserve to be given as much visibility as possible.

But is this still feasible? Isn't it already much too late? Is there still room left in Europe in the face of the conglomerate foolishness of media magnates like Silvio Berlusconi in Italy, for example, and in the Netherlands, John de Mol? Does the government dare to take public responsibility and go against the polluters of public cultural space? For it comes down to a reorganisation of that space, if we want a model that offers an exchange of ideas to replace the permanent game of chance that is presented to us today. Such a reorganisation of the cultural space will naturally be at loggerheads with the free market economy that is one of the pillars of the new Europe – which raises the question of the extent to which politicians are willing and able to create a space for quality through legislation. So far, there does not seem to be any appetite for the task. The government repeatedly says that Dutch viewers 'get what they deserve' (in the words of the Secretary of Culture) – an ominous standpoint that offers little perspective for a structural and defiant protection of quality. That it can be done otherwise has been proven by the French government, which has for years allocated a portion of the box office from American movies to its own film industry. And as I write this, today's paper reports an initiative by the French, German, Belgian, Italian and Spanish cultural institutes to open a cinema in Amsterdam for European productions. It's not much, but at least there's a concept behind it.

Equally important is the question of how to prevent such a space, once it exists, from immediately turning into a ghetto for the happy few. The answer, I believe, is as clear as it is complex: wherever 'the eye for quality' has disappeared, it must be stimulated, starting with the educational system and the mass media. There's no conceivable excuse for not doing so: after all, what we are experiencing today is the sorry result of the dictatorship of mediocrity and audience ratings. There is no cultural common ground, hardly any offering and/or recognition of quality, no cultural debate, no conceptual depth. And along with Bassam Tibi and associates, you could argue that a culture which has no common ground disintegrates of its own accord and calls down a great misfortune that goes further than culture alone. At that point, it becomes a moral and democratic duty to radically reconsider ourselves.

Jos de Putter makes documentaries and television reports. Recent films are *Dans Grozny, dans* (2002), *Wij zijn Europa* (2004) and *Passanten* (2005).

Throw Open the Shutters

Robbert Roos, the editor of *Kunstbeeld,* wrote recently that we Dutch get more from other countries than they get from us.[1] Because the Netherlands is no longer a hotspot in the international art world, he wrote, we need close ties with countries where things *are* happening. I tend to be less pessimistic. Rem Koolhaas builds the Guggenheim Hermitage museum in Las Vegas, fashion designers Viktor & Rolf are stealing the show on the Paris catwalks and Tiësto rates as the best DJ in the world. The Netherlands has a lot to offer in the field of culture. Yet Roos' argument does touch a nerve. It sometimes seems as though we have become consumed by our own little problems. In the 2005-2008 Culture Budget many internationally oriented, innovative arts organisations are in danger of losing subsidy.

I think that it would instead be to our advantage to open wide to Europe and the rest of the world. Intensive contacts with other countries are indispensable to the creative, innovative society that I envisage. When the debate about subsidies for culture was launched, I committed myself to the cause of internationally oriented cultural initiatives such as the artists' institute De Ateliers, the De Appel Foundation for Contemporary Art and the Amsterdam Dance Event. An international cultural policy is an important instrument for strengthening contacts with other countries, forming an 'umbilical cord', as Roos calls it, to art centres like London, Berlin and New York.

What should be the main aim of our international cultural policy? Should it be to put the Netherlands back on the international map? Should bridges be built between cultures? Although both are necessary, I believe in a policy of quality first, and then of listening to, and supporting, initiatives from the sector itself.

The image of the caravanserai, which Frie Leysen, the director of the *Kunstenfestival des Arts* in Brussels, uses to describe her festival, is an excellent metaphor for such an international cultural policy focused on quality.[2] The caravanserai was the great inner court where the caravans converged and deposited their baggage, and where travellers from afar ate and traded tales with each other and the inhabitants. That is what international cultural policy should be doing: enabling artists from all over the world to tell their stories, exchange experiences, and enrich each other's work.

To that end, artists should firstly be given the opportunity to travel, something that - in view of the cultural sector's limited financial means - is not always so self-evident. The HGIS resources[3] of State Secretaries Van der Laan (Culture) and Nicolaï (Foreign Affairs) and the internationalisation funds of the Mondriaan Foundation, for example, make this possible. Thus the photographer and filmmaker Liza May Post was able to hold an exhibition with the Australian artist Jan Nelson in the Sydney Museum of Contemporary Art, and Zuidelijk Toneel Hollandia was able to perform at the Avignon Theatre Festival. The challenge now is to give the opportunity to work abroad to promising young artists as well as established artists. The HGIS budget should be increased.

An international art climate can be stimulated by scrapping unnecessary rules. We should do away with the complicated registration procedures and taxes encumbering foreign artists working temporarily in the Netherlands, and abolish the quotas impeding foreign artists wanting to study at Dutch academies.

Our cultural climate can profit from the spin-off from international cultural networks established in the Netherlands, such as Manifesta for young contemporary artists or CODART for museum curators. Ties with other countries can be strengthened by investing in a rich domestic cultural climate. Advertising tycoon and art collector Charles Saatchi used his own fortune to put a new generation of British artists on the map and at one stroke made London the epicentre of the international art world again. When the National Ballet flourished under Rudi van Dantzig in the late Sixties, Rudolf Nurejev was eager to dance in the Netherlands.

The ambition to put Dutch culture back on the world map must be a realisable goal of our cultural policy. Cynics sometimes dismiss of this aspect as cheap 'Dutch promotion': the Dutch representative goes round the world with a trade agreement in one hand and clogs, tulips and Frau Antje in the other. When the architects collective MVRDV focussed so much attention on the striking Dutch pavilion at the World Exhibition in Hannover, our economy profited from it, as did our architecture's worldwide reputation. It works both ways.
Promoting Holland, however, should not overshadow the strengthening of the cultural sector. That can often lead to problems. Frank Ligtvoet, the former counsellor for Cultural Affairs in New York, describes how cultural attachés at Dutch embassies are often caught between the interests of the Ministries of Education, Culture and Science, and Foreign Affairs.[4] Foreign Affairs often regards culture as a lubricant for international relations; Education, Culture and Science promotes the interests of the cultural sector. In order to break this impasse, I feel sympathetic towards Ligvoet's proposal to make the ministries less responsible for steering the cultural attachés, who are those who carry out international cultural policy. The steering could be handed to a fund, for example, working primarily for the cultural interest. This would create the distance between government and the cultural sector that apply in other areas of cultural policy.
If you want to engage with German, French or British culture, then you can always go to those countries' cultural outposts in the Netherlands: the Goethe Institute, Maison Descartes and the British Council. The Netherlands has only one fully-fledged cultural centre abroad: the *Institut Néerlandais* in Paris, although the Flemish-Dutch House in Brussels and the Erasmus House in Jakarta have similar functions. Cultural centres can broker between cultural producers from home and abroad and strengthen interest in Dutch art. This is why Germany, France, Great Britain and the Scandinavians choose to have such representation abroad. The Netherlands could consider setting up cultural institutions in the traditional art centres of London, New York, and Berlin, as well as burgeoning Shanghai.

A third aspect of international culture policy is to establish bridges between cultures. Leaving the Nieuwe Kerk after visiting the exhibition *Morocco: 5000 years of culture* you feel that you've looked for a moment into that country's soul. The unique jewellery, carpets, costumes and manuscripts compel respect. Intensive cultural links with Morocco and Turkey could contribute to a better understanding of the culture of countries where many foreigners in the Netherlands were born. The French government has institutionalised its cultural links with the Arab world in an imposing building, the *Institut de Monde Arabe* in Paris. Such a prestigious project is not feasible in the Netherlands for the time being, but we should certainly be able to invest more in cultural links with Turkey and Morocco. The initiative for this at the moment lies with private organisations. I see a task here for the European Union, now that North Africa has become our most important neighbouring region and Turkey is seeking membership of the European Union in the long term.

The EU could do more in the area of culture. I am convinced that European states have more in common than, let's say, the Eurovision Song Festival. 'Europe is not only about markets, it is also about values and culture', announced EU chairman José Manuel Barroso recently.

European cultural policy could embrace elements similar to those I propose for Dutch policy. Lack of mobility, particularly for artists from Central and Eastern Europe, often prevents them from participating on an equal footing in cultural initiatives. A travel grants scheme for artists, comparable with the Erasmus programme for students, would be a useful initiative. Creating a 'Europe collection', whereby, analogous to the 'Netherlands collection', museums could lend objects from each other's collections more easily, would strengthen European museums in the global major league. The rules for European subsidies could be made simpler; half of the Dutch applications are currently dismissed. The Union's structural grants could be used more often for improving the cultural infrastructure of weaker regions, certainly now that research by Richard Florida (author of *The Rise of the Creative Class*) has shown how positive the effects of a rich cultural climate are on economic developments.

The European Cultural Foundation recently calculated that the Union's annual budget for culture was about 34 million euros. That's 7 cents per inhabitant, less than what the Amsterdam Muziektheater, for example, receives in subsidy every year. Considering that around 6 million European farmers together rake in billions in agricultural subsidies, I think that we should surely be able to divert a part of that to increasing the culture budget for the 3 to 4 million Europeans who work in the creative professions.

The establishment of the Prix de Rome in 1817 meant that Dutch artists were each year given the chance to travel to Rome at government's expense to find new inspiration in the 'cradle of European culture'. That first Dutch cultural policy was unambiguously internationally oriented. Lodewijk Napoleon, who created the prize, realised that international cross-pollination is essential for a flourishing cultural climate. We don't need another French occupation to give international cultural policy a prominent place again.

Boris Dittrich is the leader of the D66 parliamentary party and spokesperson for culture in the Lower House. He was responsible for the private member's bill that regulated book prices.

1 - *Kunstbeeld*, November 2004

2 - Frie Leysen was speaking on 13 February 2004 at the Nederland-Europa symposium organised by Kunsten '92 in the Rode Hoed, Amsterdam.

3 - HGIS: Homogene Groep Internationale Samenwerking (Netherlands Culture Fund)

4 - 'De Macht van de cultureel attaché'. Frank Ligtvoet in *Trouw*, 30 June 2001.

'Don't Jump on the Bandwagon – Start one Rolling Yourself'

Chris Dercon interviewed by *Sandra Jongenelen*

International cultural policy is a branch of politics, made as it is by civil servants
working under elected politicians. So you can't separate the one from the other, says
Chris Dercon (1958), director of the Haus der Kunst in Munich. Thorbecke's principle,[1]
which states that politicians have no business interfering in the content of art, is still
adhered to in Holland. While the principle is good in itself, in practice it leads to a kind
of schizophrenia – sometimes something's okay, sometimes it's not, sometimes you
have to do things one way, sometimes another. It's time the principle was given
a second look.
"Is it in fact effective? Is it being implemented correctly? Is this aloof attitude really just
sticking one's head in the sand? Shouldn't we stop pretending that politics and cultural
policy are quite separate? Oughtn't we to face up to the reality that governments are not
only responsible for cultural policy; they also put their own stamp on it in a very public
way and can later be held answerable for what they have done?
"In the second place existing instruments of policy need adjusting not only to new
domestic situations, but also to a constantly changing context abroad. For instance,
it is a fact that the Prince Claus Fund has a great influence abroad in contrast to the
Mondriaan Foundation that feels constrained to be much more passive."
Dercon hears himself speak and can't help laughing. When he talks about Holland,
he still says 'we'. "I'm from Belgium, you know", he reminds us. He has been working
in Germany for two years now, but over the past decades he has developed strong ties
with Holland. These began when he took his degree in art history at Leiden University,
after which he produced programmes on art for Dutch TV. After a period in New York
he returned to Rotterdam where he worked as the director of the Witte de With Centre
for Modern Art and subsequently the Boijmans van Beuningen Museum.
In this latter capacity in particular his policy was attacked by local politicians.
Councillors and aldermen meddled openly with his choice of artworks. For instance
one Rotterdam politician decided that the reason why Dercon exhibited a sculpture of
Adolph Hitler by Italian artist Maurizio Cattelan was to make fun of Leefbaar Rotterdam
(Liveable Rotterdam), a populist anti-immigrant party. On the basis of this accusation,
the Leefbaar Rotterdam representative wanted the council to inform Dercon's new
employer. After all, making fun of a political party by raising the issue of Nazism might
raise a few eyebrows in Germany. The exhibition had ended two years earlier and Dercon
had long since left Rotterdam, but the politician refused to let sleeping dogs lie. He was
so upset that he wanted to recoup the costs of the exhibition from Dercon personally.
In a written response the former director of Boijmans denied that he had ever made
the remark in question. "Since about 1973 I have hardly used the term if at all,
at least not in that sense (...). I should say that I don't think that making fun of people
or institutions is a very businesslike way of carrying on." The council decided not to take
any further steps, but in its response to the Leefbaar Rotterdam councillor it did make
subtle mention of the praise heaped on Dercon when he presented Cattelan's sculpture
in the Haus der Kunst. "According to the German press it is a long time since such
a "businesslike" portrayal of Hitler was on view."

There are Dutch people who think that art and politics are in the same boat. Both are in crisis and both are becoming marginalized. The domestic debate about provincialism in art is now being reported in other countries in an over-simplified form. Add to this the assassination of Pim Fortuyn and Theo Van Gogh, and it is hardly surprising that people abroad are wondering what on earth is going on in Holland. Is the country becoming culturally isolated, despite its centuries-old reputation for tolerance? With its origins as a 'free' republic, wasn't it always a country with open borders that was interested in innovation, one where cultural snobbery took a healthy form?

Dercon too notices that internationally Holland's reputation is deteriorating. "Holland urgently needs a good PR campaign", he says, "and it needs orchestrating from above because the artists lack ambition. People are afraid to stick their necks out. I'd compare the situation in Holland with that of Canada, but Canadians make a big point of escaping from the hegemony of America. The Canadian government is doing its utmost to build bridges with Europe, even to the extent of investing in commercial films. They don't make any distinction there between culture and business. The important thing is for work to have some quality and that it is non-American. I think Holland is one of the few countries left that thinks US culture is exciting. Knocking the USA is not done in Holland – something that says a lot about our own self-image."

Canada takes the spotlight and proclaims that the world needs more Canadian products. Dercon thinks we should copy Canada's example and say that the world needs more Dutch products. "For instance we lead the world in the fields of architecture and design. Everything here is aestheticized and designed. If Holland wants to exploit this phenomenon, all it needs to do is open its mouth, because we already have the necessary experience. These skills are also an export article. So we should continue to be unstinting in our support for architecture and design, even treating it like a national enterprise. In this regard cutting the subsidy for a journal like *Archis* is unforgivable."

Art and culture deserve support in hard times, but even more so in periods when they are flourishing, Dercon argues. He knows that the Dutch see this idea as paradoxical, but in his view it is basic. This is why he finds the criticism of the Mondriaan Foundation so offensive. The critics of the Mondriaan Foundation, a distribution point for government grants, argue that instead of mainly supporting artists who have already made it, they should give money to newcomers. Dercon disagrees. "With a few exceptions, their policy is very good. They don't have this attitude of treating everybody equally. If there's demand from abroad, then it needs supporting. The Dutch shouldn't think that it's enough for the demand to be created, and that everything else will follow automatically.

"You should give support precisely to those who are making it – that's what investment means. Culture *is* PR, literally and figuratively. If you want to compete internationally, cultural activities like art need support urgently. The Mondriaan Foundation should insist that its logo is on the invitations for Marlene Dumas's exhibition in the Museum of Contemporary Art in Los Angeles. Her success has a knock-on effect for other good Dutch painters.

"Isn't it strange that Dutch painting is lagging behind right now, just when painting is experiencing a huge revival as an aesthetic and commercial product? You have to do something about that, artificially or otherwise. And above all stop complaining that foreign collectors and galleries are not interested in the Dutch identity."

Dercon also has ideas about using his position abroad to support Dutch cultural products. Less than a year after he took up his post in Munich he held an exhibition of

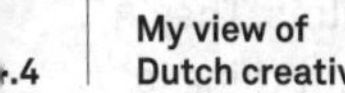

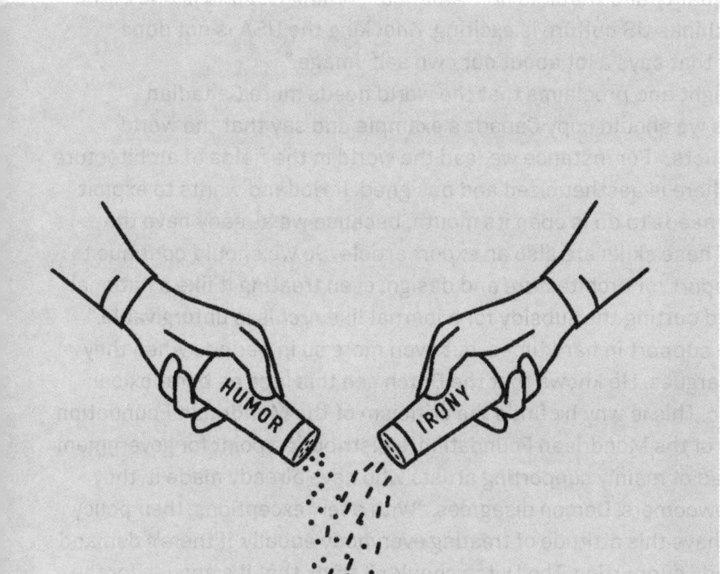

hink this is Dutch design philosophy.

egemony of America. The Canadian government is doing its utmost
Europe, even to the extent of investing in commercial films. They
nction there between culture and business. The important thing is
ne quality and that it is non-American. I think Holland is one of the
at thinks US culture is exciting. Knocking the USA is not done
ing that says a lot about our own self-image."
ootlight and proclaims that the world needs more Canadian
inks we should copy Canada's example and say that the world
roducts. "For instance we lead the world in the fields of architecture
ing here is aestheticized and designed. If Holland wants to exploit
ll it needs to do is open its mouth, because we already have the
ce. These skills are also an export article. So we should continue to
support for architecture and design, even treating it like a national
gard cutting the subsidy for a journal like *Archis* is unforgivable."
erve support in hard times, but even more so in periods when they
con argues. He knows that the Dutch see this idea as paradoxical,
asic. This is why he finds the criticism of the Mondriaan Foundation
tics of the Mondriaan Foundation, a distribution point for government
stead of mainly supporting artists who have already made it, they
o newcomers. Dercon disagrees. "With a few exceptions, their policy
n't have this attitude of treating everybody equally. If there's demand
needs supporting. The Dutch shouldn't think that it's enough for the
d, and that everything else will follow automatically.
pport precisely to those who are making it – that's what investment
R, literally and figuratively. If you want to compete internationally,
e art need support urgently. The Mondriaan Foundation should
on the invitations for Marlene Dumas's exhibition in the Museum
in Los Angeles. Her success has a knock-on effect for other good

Dutch painting is lagging behind right now, just when painting is
revival as an aesthetic and commercial product? You have to do
at, artificially or otherwise. And above all stop complaining that
d galleries are not interested in the Dutch identity."

as about using his position abroad to support Dutch cultural
a year after he took up his post in Munich he held an exhibition of

Brazil, Argentina and Chile.
Another PR tool that Holland should exploit, according to Dercon, is
a fantastic export product', he says. 'Policy in the sense of 'forecasti
hardly exists in Holland. Policy also means taking risks. Just look ho
wasted whingeing about the site and purpose of the Fotomuseum. S
to work for you and spoil them rotten. Dutch photography is a phenom
take a keen interest in."
For instance, Dercon says, the work of a designer like Hella Jongeriu
acclaimed outside Holland. The latest he heard from her was two we
lives in Rotterdam with her children and she wrote to him, "Currentl
take place within a radius of two kilometres of where I live, except fo
of whom are foreign. It's a brilliant combination." According to Dercc
she is free of all the regulations and petty squabbles that are such u
Holland and the Dutch.
Since leaving Holland, Dercon is glad to be shot of all the discussion
low culture. "That's a Dutch debate and it gets you nowhere. Neither
producers still bother about whether something is made as a comm
not. In Droog Design they tear their hair out about it. Is it high or low
we supposed to do about it? Why don't we just drop this discussion a
typical Dutch statement is that something's "too intellectual". It doe
You don't tell a pregnant woman that she's too pregnant or not pregr
Dercon sees Rem Koolhaas's plans for two towers for the Chinese TV
good PR project. During prime minister Balkenende's visit last year, '
minister, Wen Jiabao called the project an important contribution by
architecture in China. Maybe the Dutch government doesn't see it in
Dercon agrees with Wen Jiabao. "It is a Dutch export article. We shot
like Koolhaas. It is an opportunity. At the Museum of Ethnology in Le
international experts in the field of ancient Chinese art and in Amst
innovators in digital visual culture that is also a spear point in China
of the people in the Doors of Perception. Start exploiting them activ
the bandwagon – start one rolling yourself. He who hesitates is lost.
Holland has to make clear what it stands for with this PR policy. Der
architect wrote in the Spanish press about the Rijksmuseum in Ams
the first museum that you can cycle through. That's a powerful imag
image you have to take full advantage of. It's a real draw for foreigne
that, so you should adapt your publicity accordingly."

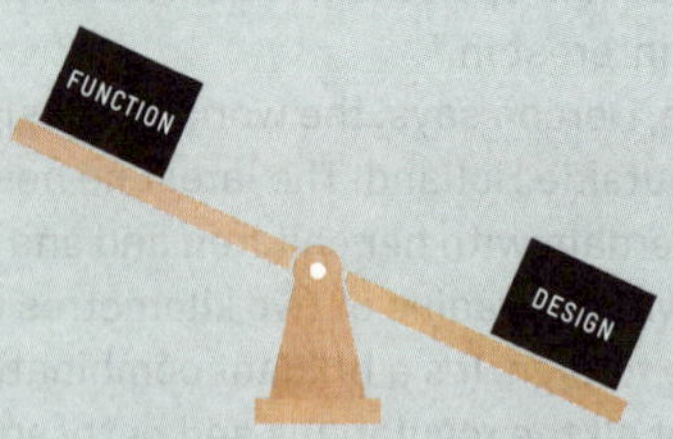

FUNCTION > DESIGN is not good.

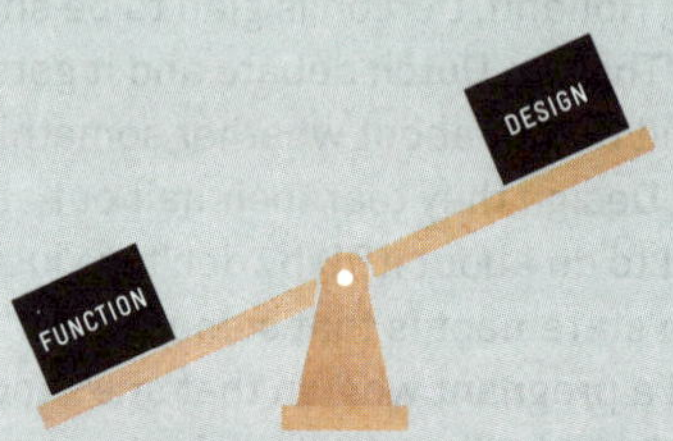

FUNCTION < DESIGN is not good.

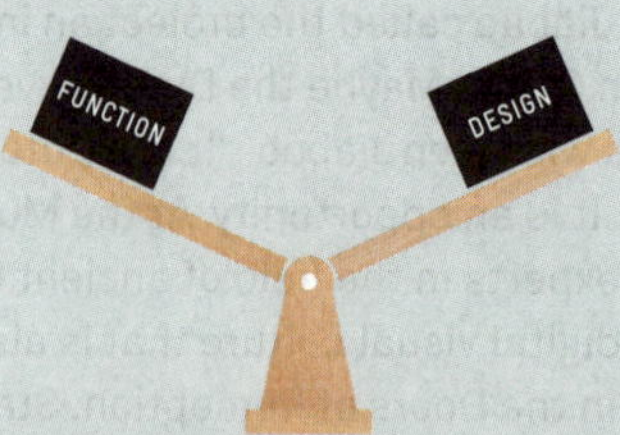

FUNCTION >< DESIGN is good!

Dutch products are like this.

the Dutch designers' collective, Droog Design. Does he see himself as an ambassador of Dutch culture? 'I feel like an ambassador of good products', he answers diplomatically. 'But the fact that these products come from Holland is a plus point. Droog Design was not particularly well known here yet now Dutch culture is doing well in Munich. Think of Harry Mulisch and Cees Nooteboom or the theatre director Johan Simons. They are good public relations for Holland. And that's important, because here in Munich there's money and influence to be won.'

Simply Droog was opened by Atzo Nicolaï, Minister of State for Europe, former arts spokesman for the Dutch right-of-centre liberal party, the VVD and ex-secretary of the Arts Council. The exhibition was made possible by Dutch money from the budget for international arts policy. The financial support the Droog products have received has enabled them to take their show on the road. After Munich it went on to museums in Brazil, Argentina and Chile.

Another PR tool that Holland should exploit, according to Dercon, is photography. "That's a fantastic export product', he says. 'Policy in the sense of 'forecasting' for the future hardly exists in Holland. Policy also means taking risks. Just look how many years were wasted whingeing about the site and purpose of the Fotomuseum. Set your own people to work for you and spoil them rotten. Dutch photography is a phenomenon that foreigners take a keen interest in."

For instance, Dercon says, the work of a designer like Hella Jongerius is widely acclaimed outside Holland. The latest he heard from her was two weeks ago. Jongerius lives in Rotterdam with her children and she wrote to him, "Currently all my activities take place within a radius of two kilometres of where I live, except for my clients, all of whom are foreign. It's a brilliant combination." According to Dercon, this means that she is free of all the regulations and petty squabbles that are such unpleasant traits of Holland and the Dutch.

Since leaving Holland, Dercon is glad to be shot of all the discussions about high and low culture. "That's a Dutch debate and it gets you nowhere. Neither the public nor the producers still bother about whether something is made as a commercial product or not. In Droog Design they tear their hair out about it. Is it high or low culture? What are we supposed to do about it? Why don't we just drop this discussion altogether. Another typical Dutch statement is that something's "too intellectual". It doesn't mean anything. You don't tell a pregnant woman that she's too pregnant or not pregnant enough."

Dercon sees Rem Koolhaas's plans for two towers for the Chinese TV building as another good PR project. During prime minister Balkenende's visit last year, the Chinese prime minister, Wen Jiabao called the project an important contribution by Holland to architecture in China. Maybe the Dutch government doesn't see it in that light, but Dercon agrees with Wen Jiabao. "It is a Dutch export article. We should exploit people like Koolhaas. It is an opportunity. At the Museum of Ethnology in Leiden there are international experts in the field of ancient Chinese art and in Amsterdam there are innovators in digital visual culture that is also a spear point in China. I'm thinking here of the people in the Doors of Perception. Start exploiting them actively. Don't jump on the bandwagon – start one rolling yourself. He who hesitates is lost."

Holland has to make clear what it stands for with this PR policy. Dercon: "A Spanish architect wrote in the Spanish press about the Rijksmuseum in Amsterdam that it is the first museum that you can cycle through. That's a powerful image, the kind of exotic image you have to take full advantage of. It's a real draw for foreigners, something like that, so you should adapt your publicity accordingly."

Every four years a new cabinet is formed, and every time this means a new round of musical chairs with the money for the arts. Most recently another Dutch PR tool was hit hard by this. The Rijksakademie in Amsterdam, with famous ex-students such as Georgina Starr and Bjarne Melgaard, was punished with a huge cut in its funding. Dercon regards this as quite inexcusable. "The Rijksakademie is an unbelievably good marketing instrument. It's better known abroad than the Stedelijk Museum in Amsterdam."

Culture is an important PR tool for a country and it can also further one's bonding with other countries. "Just think of contacts with people from immigration countries such as Turkey and Morocco. In London and Paris exoticism is a fetish, a lifestyle. That has its good and bad sides, but people don't make a huge problem of it as they do in Holland. In London and Paris, and also in Berlin, the new cultural idioms are assimilated in the cultural world in cannibalistic fashion. In Holland they are kept separate. An enormous aloofness prevails towards the new cultures and this prevents us from saying anything meaningful about them.

"Our response to them is a closed one. Erik van Lieshout's drawings of Muslims and native-born Dutch people are shown and talked about abroad with great curiosity, even in the United Emirates. In Holland you get the idea that people are not sure he really ought to be doing something like that. We are afraid of everything that's unfamiliar or that we can't pigeonhole.

"It would be interesting to compare these sharp disturbing drawings of Van Lieshout with a bad, melodramatic film like Submission by Hirsi Ali and Theo van Gogh. You don't need to be a sociologist to do that; it's a job for an art critic. The only one who does this in Holland is Anna Tilroe, and no one exactly thanks her for it. That's because recent Dutch art criticism has mainly been concerned with Holland.

"In Holland they're also always talking about authenticity. At the exhibition *Unpacking Europe* in Boijmans in 2002 many people thought the art was behind the times, that it imitated us and wasn't authentic. That's something you often hear about the activities the Prince Claus Fund supports. But there's no such thing as authenticity any more. So much has been filtered and there are so many different varieties of modernism now, each with its own tempo. Think about it a minute – Dutch culture is also not authentic, and hasn't been for a long time either.

"A large part of the Dutch cultural elite has been making remarkably conservative statements recently that aren't all that different from what you hear in the political arena or the media. That's because people have become too inward-looking. You should make a point of inviting 'the other' and 'others', for instance people and products from abroad to enquire about your own expectations and if need be to subvert them. That's culture too and an expression of culture."

Sandra Jongenelen is a freelance journalist for *Het Financieele Dagblad* and *Kunstbeeld*, and a member of the advisory council for *Boekman*, a journal for art, culture and policy.

1 - Johan Rudolf Thorbecke, liberal statesman, three times Prime Minister of Holland, chief author of the Dutch constitution of 1848.

Culture and
Economics

Dutch cultural policy is in the first place directed toward artistic quality. Beyond that, the striking thing about the political debate on culture in the Netherlands is that Dutch politicians have from time immemorial been obsessed by public support for art. Not surprisingly, the various legitimizations for Dutch art policy that were in vogue over the past decades changed in synchronicity with changes in the spirit of the times, without the necessity of an unhampered, autonomous development of the arts ever coming up for discussion. A lot of flirting with the economic aspect of culture went on, naturally, but the love affair usually did not go much further than that.

In international cultural policy, which in the Netherlands mirrors national policy, terms like competition, profit, import and export are likewise avoided. Beyond our borders too, we primarily want to be able to show our best side without thinking about getting rich. What's more, we are even prepared to invest heavily in international cultural profiling. The quality, creativity and innovation of Dutch culture are often praised, partly as a result of this. At the same time, as several contributors to this section point out, the Netherlands is insufficiently capable of plucking the economic fruits of that praise. Take Dutch fashion, for instance. In the early and mid nineties, two generations of talented designers stormed the catwalks in Paris and filled the fashion magazines. Only a few of them proved able to turn their talent into profitable businesses as independent designers. A successful show in Paris might lead to an order, but designers usually didn't have the production facilities to carry it out. Another example can be found in the new media. In her contribution to this section, Femke Wolting observes that in the games field, the Netherlands originally missed the boat because the gap between art and commerce was too big.

In the economic sense, fashion and games belong in the category of cultural products, just as do much of the visual arts, design, literature and architecture: tangible objects which can be sold. There is certainly profit to be made in this area. But this is also true for the category of cultural services: art forms which are presented and 'consumed' live, such as the performing arts. The essays in this section examine the various ways to forge a relationship between the two.

The creative industry is receiving more and more attention in the Netherlands. Culture plays a crucial role in the knowledge economy, declares Joeri van den Steenhoven. "Identity and meaning are increasingly regarded as key factors in creating economic value for both products and services. This is most noticeable in the creative industries." Culture and economy can be directly linked: economic activities with a cultural component can help strengthen a country or region's international competitive position. "Four factors are involved: developing talent, stimulating innovation, creating fertile environments for creativity and promoting the creative industry." Which the Finns have done for years, and now they are reaping the benefits.

Rick van der Ploeg also believes that competition will play a greater role in both the importing and exporting of cultural products and that this can have a positive effect on the quality of Dutch culture. As examples of countries that have successfully incorporated culture in their national branding, he cites France, Denmark, Austria and, again, Finland.

Dutch design must not be forced into an economic straitjacket, argues Peik Suyling. "Dutch design is a uniquely strong, conceptual cultural statement. It must not be treated as a cash cow. To do so is to negate everything Dutch design stands for." Instead, we must do what we are good at: explore new territory. It is possible, for instance, to employ design in complex problem areas that are normally outside the designer's sphere of activity. Until recently, people thought in terms of solutions; nowadays processes are more important, and the focus is on the border areas between diverse perspectives, in the approach to a problem. Design can play an important role in the finding and framing of solutions in these areas. People must work closely together on this, but designers are used to that.

Mir Wermuth examines the world of Dutch rock and pop music and observes that this is a sector where commerce and governmental support exist side-by-side. Both parties also promote the sector internationally, with an eye to the music's commercial potential. The biggest success until now has been Dutch dance music, although there is nothing Dutch about it, according to Wermuth.

Femke Wolting points out a growing international trend: a transitional zone between artistic experiments and the games that are only produced to make money. She believes that it is time for artistically inclined game makers in the Netherlands to close the gap between autonomous art and commerce by looking further than the small in-crowd of the art world and focusing on a wider audience. Separate financing models are necessary for this: producing new media costs a lot of money and requires an integrated policy by the Department of Economic Affairs, the Ministry of Education, Cultural Affairs and Science, and the Department of Finance.

The essays in this section offer several possibilities for a fruitful cross-fertilization between culture and the economy. They also reveal that current Dutch government policy makes no connection between economics and culture. Perhaps the government's proposed Culture and Economy memorandum will bring a change in this. It seems useful, in any case, to make a distinction between culture's economic aspect, which should be given an appropriate role in cultural policy, and the economy's cultural aspect, which should become a vital component of economic policy. At the moment I'm not really sure whether this should necessarily lead to marriage – and certainly not marriage with community property – but an LAT relationship would be exciting enough for the time being.

George Lawson has been the director of the International Cultural Activities Foundation since 2004. Prior to that, he headed up the cultural department of the Dutch embassy in Berlin, was deputy director of the arts for the Ministry of Education, Cultural Affairs and Science and held positions as director of the Schouwburg, the Centrum Beeldende Kunst, and the Ro Theater in Rotterdam.

Culture and the Creative Economy

In much of Europe the market and the arts are unhappy bedfellows. Art critics suggest that only subsidised symphony orchestras and classical music ensembles perform good music. Commercial orchestras may be adequate for accompanying musicals, operettas and the popular operas but not difficult or contemporary music. Similarly, subsidised theatre stages the artistically valuable theatre repertoire and commercial theatre concentrates on lighter stuff such as comedy, cabaret or Christmas pantomimes. Commercial culture offers many marvels. Even Shakespeare wrote for the people's theatre and managed to pull in the crowds in a fiercely competitive environment. Contemporary Europe has excellent museums that flourish without subsidy. The quality of some commercial theatre productions is at least as good as those of subsidised theatre groups. A growing number of cultural entrepreneurs cherish their autonomy and succeed without subsidy.

Subsidised culture loses significance unless it reaches out to new and more diverse audiences, since it now caters largely for white, highly educated audiences and not for the huge influx of immigrants. Culture pessimists detest the money-oriented, culturally impoverished way people live. They fear that market forces dumb down expressions of high culture to get mass attention and warn that high culture is not entertainment. Economists stress that the market produces plenty of cultural niches for the elite and low culture for the majority (Cowen, 1998).[1] Globalisation, the Internet and other technical innovations allow economies of scale and enable the market to produce diversity and variety. Some prefer not to waste public money on culture at all, because this only serves the self-centred interests of the members of a passionate minority (Grampp, 1989).[2] Of course, if key persons in culture waste their time and energy on lobbying and trying to get the maximum subsidy, less is left for cultural production. The state-driven systems of France and Italy are not transparent, and are prone to political or bureaucratic favouritism and bias towards prestige objects. The UK adopts an arms-length approach with an independent Arts Council and no ministerial responsibility. It suffers less from these problems, but may focus too much on 'art for art's sake' as the government has little influence on the way cultural subsidies are allocated. The Dutch arms-length approach of an independent Arts Council is combined with ministerial responsibility and has the advantage that the minister can set broad priorities and criteria that the Arts Council has to adhere to without trying to influence artistic judgements, but it is much more prone to lobbying. Stimulating demand across the board (e.g., with tax incentives) carries little danger of lobbying, but suffers from dead-weight losses and bias towards middle-of-the-road culture. Arts Councils usually have to use 'quality' as the prime criteria. But who decides what 'quality' is? Is it only the Western canon of established high culture?

Cultural experiences

—

Cultural experiences like pay-TV or visits to the performing arts or museums are rival goods. Prices then reflect true costs and the market functions well. If enjoyment of a cultural experience does not reduce the benefits derived by other persons, it is non-

rival. But noisy, uninterested audiences destroy the enjoyment of interested art lovers.
Though it is feasible to use jamming to exclude people from non-rival cultural goods
such as radio or TV broadcasts, it makes no economic sense. Everybody wants a free
ride on non-rival cultural goods, hence subsidies for open-channel radio and TV
seem warranted. Open-channel TV is a public good, but pay-TV is a rival and excludable
private good and so the government should restrict itself to competition policy. If
congestion costs are large, cultural experiences may no longer be non-rival.
For example, the congestion cost imposed by the marginal visitor to the British Museum
is eight pounds; to this should be added the costs of security, maintenance, cleaning,
etc. Free admissions may thus be harmful. Sometimes it is not feasible to exclude
those who do not pay. This may happen with the restoration of a listed building or
a magnificent design by world-famous architects; think of the impact of the Centre
Beaubourg, designed by Renzo Piano and Richard Rogers, on the depressed Les Halles
area. Since passers-by can neither be asked for a fee nor excluded from enjoying well-
maintained heritage or splendid architecture, the market under-provides such non-
rival, non-excludable public goods. The performing arts are excludable private goods
and thus do not deserve the relatively large subsidies they get (De Grauwe, 1990).[3]
However, language is a public good and this may justify support. This may also be true
for drama, literature and film.
Rapid technological changes have altered the nature of cultural goods in a big way.
Today many get their favourite music from illegal websites. CDs were once rival (private)
goods, but are now non-rival (public) goods. This shift threatens the livelihood of the
recording industry. There is a market for mass-produced posters of Da Vinci's Mona
Lisa, Van Gogh's Sunflowers and Vermeer's Milkmaid, because poster producers pay
author rights and guarantee quality. This is not so easy for musicians whose artistic
products are taken for free from the net, hence extra income from concerts, books,
interviews and merchandise will be more important to them. Still, technological
developments, E-culture and lower costs of transport and communication have led
to an unprecedented democratisation of culture. The Internet and new technology
have lowered prices and raised speed, which in turn has increased participation in,
and accessibility to both classical and contemporary art. The increase in possibilities
and the speed at which one can travel and transport art objects makes expositions
of even unique art objects available to a growing number of people throughout the
world. Libraries, archives, museums and performing arts are showing their treasures
increasingly on television or Internet. Although many feared that virtual displays would
undermine the demand for the real thing, this turned out to be unjustified. There is also
a shift from autonomous to applied arts. In fact, the economy increasingly relies on
products of commercial and subsidised industries as diverse as film, radio, television,
advertising, design of household products, web design, architecture, fashion, music,
publishing and festivals. Culture generates positive spin-offs as a flourishing cultural
climate pulls in tourism and new businesses. Well-preserved listed buildings, good
architecture and thriving performance arts make cities attractive for businesses,
scarce knowledge workers and tourists (Florida, 2002).[4]
High culture has snob appeal (Bourdieau, 1979).[5] As soon as the rest of the population
starts appreciating it, the elite loses interest. Still, the government should ensure
that more people enjoy high culture. In fact, a Danish study shows that 82 per cent
of non-users of the Royal Theatre would be willing to pay; many people are happy to
support the arts that they themselves do not visit. Non-visitors may derive pleasure

Essay by Rick van der Ploeg

from reading critical reviews or watching television recordings of opera performances, value the derived benefits for television, the film industry, cultural education, cultural heritage and traditions, or cherish the international prestige. Rich people face a higher cost for high culture than poorer people, since the cost of visiting, say, opera is the ticket plus travel costs and foregone income. They are thus less sensitive to the price of the ticket, so can be charged more.

Convincing arguments for subsidising culture
—

In my 1999 White Paper *Culture as Confrontation* (*Uitgangspunten voor het Cultuurbeleid 2001-2004*) I set out why government should support culture. First, there is a strong case for investment in cultural awareness and cultural education of children to help them develop a taste for cultural experiences that leave a lasting impression. With vouchers children can each year go four to six times to a concert or opera, museum, film, theatre or dance performance, which allows them choose for themselves what they want to experience. In addition, cultural organisations may be subsidised to develop cultural experiences for young people. The reason for promoting cultural education is that high culture is only fully appreciated if people are exposed to it at an early age. For many children cultural education is their only chance to develop an awareness of, and taste for, high culture.

Second, there are ways of bringing high culture to a broader range of people. Subsidized high culture is primarily enjoyed by older, greying, white, highly educated people. By bringing high culture to public parks, pop temples, libraries, community halls and shopping precincts, one reaches out to new and more diverse audiences. This yields interesting experiences in the twilight zone between high and low culture and forces the arts to make their output more of a non-rival, non-excludable good and less of a luxury good.

Third, there is a case for stimulating demand rather than supply. In the Netherlands there has been a shift from subsidising supply of contemporary visual arts towards subsidising demand (through subsidies on the interest paid on loans to purchase the work of living artists). In the performing arts a greater emphasis on the demand side is also needed. Many venues in the provinces have a tendency to program standard fare in order to break even. There is thus a case for Programming Funds, whose mission is to reward those venues that come with an adventurous, high quality program of culture. It takes time to cultivate an audience and make it worthwhile for successful productions to have a longer run. A 'bums on seats' premium for the performing arts may also improve incentives for drawing bigger audiences.

Fourth, the market fails to deliver sufficient non-rival and/or non-excludable cultural experiences. Cultural experiences also generate social cultural capital, which benefits society at large and not only the few who attend. Government should support these with subsidies, tax incentives, regulation or public sector provision. The sum of the marginal benefits of cultural experiences must equal the cost. Making culture more widely available may make people work less and pay fewer taxes. This erosion of the tax base raises the cost of culture. If culture attracts highly skilled workers, businesses and tourists, it raises tax revenues and the cost is lower.

Fifth, government may subsidise cultural artefacts of intergenerational value, especially if they are on display to the public. Think of restoration and maintenance of historic churches, farms, castles, bridges and locks, landscapes or archives,

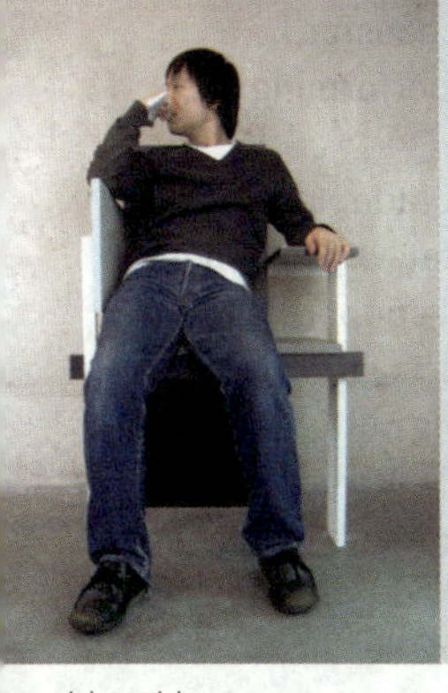

etveld and I.

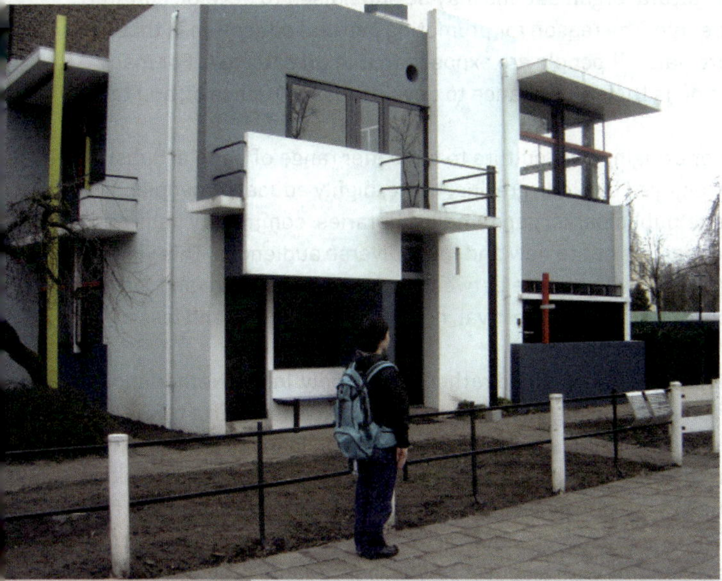

cultural experiences that leave a lasting impression. With vouchers
ar go four to six times to a concert or opera, museum, film, theatre
ce, which allows them choose for themselves what they want to
ion, cultural organisations may be subsidised to develop cultural
ng people. The reason for promoting cultural education is that high
appreciated if people are exposed to it at an early age. For many
ucation is their only chance to develop an awareness of, and taste

ays of bringing high culture to a broader range of people. Subsidized
arily enjoyed by older, greying, white, highly educated people.
ture to public parks, pop temples, libraries, community halls and
one reaches out to new and more diverse audiences. This yields
ces in the twilight zone between high and low culture and forces
ir output more of a non-rival, non-excludable good and less of

e for stimulating demand rather than supply. In the Netherlands
ft from subsidising supply of contemporary visual arts towards
(through subsidies on the interest paid on loans to purchase the
). In the performing arts a greater emphasis on the demand side is
enues in the provinces have a tendency to program standard fare
en. There is thus a case for Programming Funds, whose mission is
ues that come with an adventurous, high quality program of culture.
vate an audience and make it worthwhile for successful
a longer run. A 'bums on seats' premium for the performing arts
centives for drawing bigger audiences.
ails to deliver sufficient non-rival and/or non-excludable cultural
al experiences also generate social cultural capital, which benefits
not only the few who attend. Government should support these
ncentives, regulation or public sector provision. The sum of the
cultural experiences must equal the cost. Making culture more
y make people work less and pay fewer taxes. This erosion of the
cost of culture. If culture attracts highly skilled workers, businesses
s tax revenues and the cost is lower.
ay subsidise cultural artefacts of intergenerational value,
e on display to the public. Think of restoration and maintenance
farms, castles, bridges and locks, landscapes or archives,

libraries, museums and archaeological treasures. Each of these adds to the social stock of cultural capital and, if they deteriorate, harm is done to the welfare of future generations. Even if one never visits certain parts of the country, one does not want the heritage in those parts to go to the dogs. This may be true for opera as well. It may also motivate funding experiment and research and development.

Sixth, failures on the supply side may merit temporary subsidy. This is the infant-industry argument. UNESCO points out that Tibetan horn players, Balinese dancers and Cape Verdian singers have unique selling points, which can be popularized through the global media, CDs, DVDs and live performances. These artists can help brand their own countries, like the Beatles and Abba did, and thus boost their economies. Another example is that people working in the applied arts often reject income subsidies, preferring help that will empower them to make a living from the market. Avant garde cultural activities find it harder to borrow money than more profitable, run-of-the-mill cultural activities, so the government might usefully supply risk-bearing capital and fiscal incentives. Interest rate incentives may induce private citizens to provide money in the form of soft loans.

Unconvincing arguments for subsidizing culture

—

Some argue that demand for cultural goods depends on their supply and that the government should therefore subsidize supply. However, it is better to boost demand for high culture through cultural education, vouchers, reaching out to new and more diverse audiences, and programming subsidies. Another fallacious argument is that culture should be affordable for everyone. The sensible response is to use price discrimination (e.g. asking season ticket holders to pay more per seat than those who buy last-minute individual tickets) or to boost demand among lower incomes or children through education, vouchers, action programs or other means. If one is concerned about a tendency to cater to middle-of-the-road taste at the expense of avant garde culture, teachers and the managers of venues may be encouraged to gently cultivate a taste for high culture. Yet another unconvincing argument is that price increases lead to even bigger falls in demand and thus to a fall in revenues, making subsidies essential. But demand is often inelastic, in which case raising prices will boost revenues. If venues are not fully utilized, then it's demand that should be boosted, not supply. It is often argued that culture is produced under decreasing average costs, so subsidy is needed to ensure full utilization of venues. This is pretty unconvincing. If venues do not pull in audiences, they can experiment with cheap last-minute tickets and marketing. There may be a case for stimulating demand through education, vouchers, action plans and programming subsidies, not for extra supply subsidies. Many argue mistakenly that culture contributes to employment, but in a tight labour market there is no economic need for this. The freedom to educate oneself as an artist does not oblige the government to provide for enough orchestras, theatre companies, etc. to employ all arts graduates. The employment argument may be valid for certain professions (e.g. restoration), where valuable skills might otherwise be lost for future generations. The fact that many artists are poor is not a valid argument either, because we should subsidize all poor people regardless of their occupation.

In the arts there is not much scope for improvements in productivity, so its relative price increases (Baumol and Bowen, 1966)[6] and greater pressure for subsidies result. However, the newly-found riches of technical progress imply that people willingly spend a greater part of their budgets on the arts. In addition, there may be a shift from unique to reproductive, small- to large-scale, and labour-extensive to labour-intensive productions.

International cultural policy: different approaches in Europe
—

National pride demands that each country promote its own culture abroad, implying a gain of mutual respect on all sides. Cultural diplomacy may help to win foreign contracts for home enterprises. The UK seems to place the greatest emphasis on economic interest. If this is the case, international cultural policy formulation is a by-product of foreign policy and has little to do with inducing a thriving international cultural exchange. If the initiative lies with the Minister of Culture, priority may go to the dissemination of high culture rather than popular expressions of culture geared towards other motives than showcasing. There may also be more emphasis on foreign culture, which could be Third World music, Berber culture or Bombay films (Denmark, France, Sweden, Netherlands) in addition to the Western canon. This added diversity has intrinsic value and encourages competition at home. Indeed, some countries showcase the best foreign young visual artists, film directors, architects, and musicians if they are better than homegrown talent. Not all countries agree, notably France. Promotion of Swedish and French music abroad is successful. In France music sales abroad rose from 1.5 million units in 1992 to 39 million units in 2000. Still, the French probably regard this spectacular growth as insufficient to counter the dominance of the Anglo-Saxon music industry. The French also promote their film, TV and radio abroad, again with some success. The Danish Dogma group has met with success abroad while Finland obtains similar results in music, design and dance. Not only Britain is trying to promote a 'cool' image. Austria works on a modern image too (witness Kruder and Dorfmeister). Both countries make use of branding, corporate identities and joint marketing approaches to promote their culture abroad.
Some countries empower artists to compete in international markets (UK, Netherlands). Others, led by France, disagree and practice cultural protectionism. Special economic instruments to promote sales of French films, books or music outside France offer ethnic minorities the chance to express their culture, or bring in non-European culture. This makes sense, but keeping US and other foreign cultures out does not. There may be a case for promoting own-language products, but not for blocking foreign-language products.

Conclusion
—

High culture faces the danger of becoming marginalized as the leisure industry becomes ever more professional, the young invest less in cultural competence, the circle of genuine art lovers becomes smaller, audiences become more diverse, and culture is increasingly restricted to places of entertainment. Governments fight dumbing down by ensuring that culture is more than mere amusement, invest in talent and education, and make space for innovation and experiment. They should avoid addiction to cultural subsidies and the status quo and not discriminate against newcomers. In the Renaissance there was fierce competition between producers of art. Now a healthy gust of domestic and foreign competition and more market-oriented support from governments can be important motors behind a revival of the creative and innovative cultural sectors of Europe.

Rick van der Ploeg is a professor of economics at the European University Institute in Florence, and the University of Amsterdam. He is also a member of the UNESCO World Heritage Committee. He was the Netherlands' State Secretary for Culture and Media from 1998 to 2002.

1 - Cowen, T. (1998): *In Praise of Commercial Culture* (Harvard University Press, Cambridge, Ma.).

2 - Grampp, W.D. (1989): Pricing the Priceless – Art, Artists and Economics (Basic Books, New York).

3 - Grauwe, P. de (1990): De Nachtwacht in het Donker (Lannoo, Tielt).

4 - Florida, R. (2002): *The Rise of the Creative Class* (Basic Books, New York).

5 - Bourdieu, P. (1979): *La distinction – critique sociale due jugement* (Editions de Minuit, Paris).

6 - Baumol, W.J. and W.G. Bowen (1966): *Performing Arts – The Economic Dilemma* (Twentieth Century Fund,Cambridge, Mass.).

Culture and Economics

Essay by Rick van der Ploeg

Building Creative Capital

In the knowledge economy, economic, technological, social and cultural trends meet and interact. Information and communications technology has fundamentally changed the ways in which we live and work. In recent years, many commentators have examined the relationship between technology and the economy. We are now beginning to realise that the cultural dimension is lacking.

Culture is crucial to the knowledge economy. Identity and meaning are increasingly regarded as key factors in creating economic value for both products and services. This is most noticeable in the creative industries, defined in the United Kingdom in 1997 as "economic activities which have their origin in individual creativity, skill and talent and which have a potential for wealth and job creation through the generation and exploitation of intellectual property." In the Netherlands an estimated 3% of the population works in the creative industry, rising to 7% in the Amsterdam region. In that region one out of ten new jobs is created in this sector. There is obvious growth potential here.

The cultural dimension is also important for the rest of the economy. The value of an increasing number of products and services is determined by their design and by the experience they invoke. Whether it be clothing, cars, or anything else, the distinguishing factor for many products is not function, but form. This also determines a growing proportion of production costs. Moreover, we are spending more and more of our income on services like entertainment, culture and leisure activities. And in the broader sense, culture - as the domain for expression, reflection and exchange - is increasingly the context in which social and economic developments derive their value.

Politicians and policy makers are starting to realise that the economy's cultural aspect is becoming more important. The Dutch government is currently preparing a memorandum on culture and the economy. The Innovation Platform, a government advisory body headed by Prime Minister Balkenende, has singled out the creative industry as one of the key sectors in the future economy of the Netherlands. In many places, the concept of the 'creative city' is being discussed. A focus on the cultural dimension can be seen in other countries. Until now, however, linking culture with the economy has proven difficult - let alone deciding how to translate this into policy.

It is therefore important to determine exactly what connection there is between the two. This essay is a briefing on how to connect culture with the economy, and what policies are necessary to achieve this. There are two types of linkages. First, a direct connection, comprised of economic activities with a cultural component that can contribute to the strengthening of a nation or region's competitive position on the international market. Second, an indirect connection in which the public value of culture is the central factor. In an economy and a society that are both increasingly becoming dependent on creativity and innovation, culture is patently indispensable; a strong arts and cultural sector, lively cultural facilities and a society that accepts innovation and diversity are essential. Both are important factors in attracting business to countries and regions, as authors like Richard Florida have shown. Both types of connection are important. The forging of such connections can be seen as building creative capital, which society

must encourage to be able to benefit fully from the knowledge economy.
The focus in this essay will nonetheless be on the first, direct, connection. Four factors are involved: developing talent, stimulating innovation, creating fertile environments for creativity and promoting the creative industry. For these factors possible policies are being examined, based on examples from Finland, as that country has successfully been engaged in exploiting culture in its economy for years. Finally, we will formulate several challenges for Dutch cultural policy as it creates connections between culture and the economy in years to come.

Talent
—

The single most important resource of the knowledge economy is talent. The creativity and skills with which people turn new ideas and insights into products and services to a large degree determines the power of a developed society such as ours. And indeed, investing in human capital is at the basis of all government strategy. This includes investing in education to build a strong basis and the encouragement of excellence in specific areas of education and research. Finland has done both consistently in the past decade. Over the years, its expenditure on education has risen to one of the highest levels in the EU, and it has founded numerous institutions of higher education, many of them for the arts. The University for Art and Design in Helsinki, with its 1700 students (14% of whom are foreigners) and 400 teachers, has become the largest art institution in Scandinavia and has earned great international respect. Not surprisingly, the selection threshold is high. Of the 2000 annual applicants only 9% are admitted. When we look at talent development in the Netherlands, the general picture is bleak. We spend far less on education than do our neighbours, which leads to lower participation in education and offers less room for excellence. A relative exception, however, is art education. This is held in high international esteem, and the art schools draw in a lot of international talent. It is worth noting that unlike the rest of Dutch higher education, admission is based on selection. This provides a good starting point, but it does not mean that we should be satisfied with the situation. The combination of higher student participation and excellence in specific areas requires intensified effort, which even more than previously must be aimed at top quality. If this doesn't happen, the Netherlands will have a less attractive climate for international companies in the creative industries than other countries. Companies in the games industry, for example, complain about the shortage of highly educated talent here. They are forced to import this talent from abroad, making them question whether it wouldn't be better to move elsewhere themselves.

Innovation
—

The next factor is innovation. This means stimulating new products and services by investing in research and development. This is also true for cultural products and services. For example, in 2000 Finland started the Design 2005 programme, with the goal of making Finland an internationally leading country in the area of design by 2005. Finnish companies in numerous sectors are challenged to link up with designers and find out what design can mean for them. As part of this programme, the Finnish innovation agency Tekes started an Industrial Design Technology Programme which stimulates product development through design applications and then helps to put the results on the international market. €30 million has been invested in this so far. At the same time, the Finnish Academy started an Industrial Design Research Programme in order to strengthen more basic research in the area of design. Although the Netherlands does have several well regarded institutions and research groups in this field, a specifically directed programme with considerable financial backing like that of Design 2005 does not exist. Moreover, it should be noted that Tekes functions in a manner totally different to its Dutch counterpart SenterNovem.

Crossovers
—

Networks are essential to the information society. Many successful innovations stem from the unforeseen combinations and reactions that occur when different domains and organisations come in contact with each other. Crossovers thus become the key to innovation in the information society. For government policy, this means that the core of an innovation strategy lies in those places in the economy and society where these sort of crossovers can arise. The challenge we face is to create the conditions which will stimulate these crossovers.
Finland has achieved this in several ways. One example is the International Design Business Management programme. In this educational and research programme, institutions such as the Helsinki School of Economics, The University of Art and Design Helsinki, and the Helsinki University of Technology collaborate to make design a more integrated part of the operational management of Finnish companies. Another example is the Media Centre Lume, founded in 1999, where students, researchers, and companies in various creative disciplines come together. The centre is affiliated with the University of Art and Design and located in Arabiarantia, a district of Helsinki which is being developed into a hotspot for the creative industry. Here, all factors come together: education, research and a fertile business environment.
In the Netherlands, we see that some cities are indeed looking for similar approaches, but since they rarely seek to combine all factors. The result is mostly restyled old-industrial buildings for new creative companies but that have little connection with education and research. However, moves in the right direction are being made in the Strijp-S district in Eindhoven, which is intended to become a breeding ground for design and technology, with Philips Design and the Design Academy as the main player. Up till now, the Netherlands has had very few programmes in the area of education or research that connect culture and the economy. This is the result of a prevailing conviction that culture must be autonomous. Just as in the sciences, interaction with commercial companies is considered inappropriate. This is a serious misconception, because in more and more countries we see the emergence of programmes and schools that have successfully combined Art with Business.

Promotion
—

Developing talent, stimulating innovation, and fostering crossovers: fine, but not enough. The final challenge is to show what the creative industry has to offer. This entails actively promoting the creative areas in which a nation or region shines and demonstrating what that can mean to national companies and international markets. Finland has been doing this for years in the field of design. This first occurs, of course, through the products and services themselves; they must prove their worth. But it is also possible to give general support. The Design Forum Finland was set up in 1989 to promote Finnish design, both within Finland and internationally. Another example is the English language magazine Form Function Finland, which has promoted Finnish design since 1980 and is now distributed in over 70 countries. In addition, numerous activities have been developed with the aim of promoting Finnish design in foreign journals and at international conferences. The Netherlands, too, has various successes in this sphere, but most are the fruit of isolated private initiatives. This is not wrong in itself, but their effectiveness could be much greater with government support. We lack a consistent strategy. Too often the Netherlands still profiles itself as the land of cheese, windmills and tulips - whereas in fact it has far more to offer.

In Conclusion

—

Finland is now reaping the benefit of a long-term strategy to help develop a particular sector into a creative industry: design. Begun in the 1980s, this policy was intensified around the turn of the millennium. In the Netherlands, preconditions for the development of certain sectors of the creative industry also exist. We have international top players in industrial design, new media and architecture, and the potential to develop them. But that requires daring: we must pick out a number of specific fields in which we want to invest in talent development, innovation, crossovers and promotion. These certainly need not be the same areas as Finland promotes - preferably not, in fact. We must rely on our own strengths and uniqueness. But if the Netherlands wants to stimulate the creative industry, it will be necessary to choose the areas that have a chance in international markets and concentrate on developing those. Therefore the cultural sector has to stop thinking that economics is a dirty word and accept the idea that economic cultural policy is essential alongside traditional cultural policy – that's 'alongside', mind you, not 'in place of'. The new policy will relate to other criteria, such as the contribution to employment opportunity and economic growth. Next, teachers and researchers in cultural and economics departments will have to collaborate with each other more than they do now, as is already happening in other countries. The government needs to develop policies that foster new crossovers between culture and the economy and promote them, so that a number of sectors within the creative industry - certainly not all - can flourish at an international level. That is really building creative capital.

Joeri van den Steenhoven is cofounder of the independent think tank Knowledgeland, and member of the Lisbon Council. In March 2005 he organised the international conference 'Creative Capital'.

Who is the Johan Cruyff of Dutch Rock 'n' Roll?
Mir Wermuth interviewed by *Sandra Jongenelen*

Listen to an international discussion about architecture and inevitably the name Rem Koolhaas is mentioned. If seventeenth-century painters are discussed then inevitably the name of Rembrandt will be heard, and if football is your subject then it's not long before the name Johan Cruyff crops up. But with pop music? Who are Dutch rock 'n' roll icons known around the world?

"Unfortunately," says Mir Wermuth, Director of Education at the Faculty of Communication and Journalism in Utrecht and member of the board of the Dutch Rock & Pop Institute in Amsterdam, "compared to architecture and design, Dutch pop music is somewhere near the bottom. Koolhaas is asked to do masterclasses, but that'll never happen with anyone from the Dutch pop music industry. You can't imagine Barry Hay, the lead singer in Golden Earring, getting any sort of invitation. The British and the Americans have it all to themselves."

This insignificant position is due to the fact that Dutch pop and rock music is not very distinctive. "Our music happens in English, is aimed at the hit parade, and makes little impression on the international music market. Internationally, Dutch pop music is on the up and up both commercially and aesthetically, but the successes are still extremely modest," explains Wermuth, who three years ago obtained her doctoral degree with a thesis on the popularisation of hiphop culture in Europe.

What appears impossible within pop is normal for dance music. The Dutch DJ Tiësto – the stage name of Thijs Verwest – has already stood as number one in the world for a number of years. He has toured in Europe, Asia, and North and South America, produces albums, he won almost all the important dance music prizes last year, and took part in the opening ceremony of the Olympic Games in Athens, where he played live for ninety minutes in front of more than seventy thousand people in the stadium and an audience of many millions of television viewers around the world.

Wermuth suspects that Tiësto's popularity is due to the fact that he comes over as an ordinary boy-next-door. "He doesn't have any starlike airs and there's no suggestion of drugs around him. He's really a boy in jeans and a T-shirt and that appeals to people. Everyone wants to dance and flirt to his joyful music."

Wermuth finds it surprising that Tiësto has been able to maintain his international position for so many years. No Dutch rock musician has ever experienced even a fraction of the DJ's following. Tiësto has got to where he is without any government subsidy worth mentioning. "And he's appreciated artistically. Dance music is judged internationally according to the same quality standards as rock."

The Dutch dance DJs Armin van Buren and Junkie XL also score well internationally. The musician Tom Holkenborg, alias Junkie XL, lives in America. He switches between rock and dance music and makes music for Microsoft's Xbox computer games and commercials for sports fashion giant Nike.

House music is just seventeen. Compared to painting, classical music, and architecture, pop music is a youngster, turning fifty last year. The official birth date of rock 'n' roll, the fifth of July 1954, is the day of Elvis Presley's first professional recording session.

Most pop music half a century later is still imported from the US. American and British music continues to dominate the Dutch market. "America's the top, but for the Dutch it's unreachable," Wermuth acknowledges. "Till now not a single Dutch entertainer has managed to build up a long-term career in the US. Anouk had the potential to be successful in America, but failed to fulfil it on her first tour. It's almost impossible to survive that amount of damage."
Dutch pop music can claim some successes. Songs like Shocking Blue's 'Venus' and Golden Earring's 'Radar Love' belong to the international canon of iconic pop music. But nobody knows that these hits were by Dutch bands. That's not so strange; what's Dutch about them? What is Dutch about DJ Tiësto? Only his attitude of 'just be normal' is typically Dutch. There is nothing Dutch about his music.
The lack of a Dutch identity is characteristic of our country's pop music, says Wermuth. "Our music is not meant as a vehicle of language and culture, as it is in France. Nor does it have something of its own, as in Belgium and Sweden for example. Abba had a quality very much their own; something distinctly North European."
The lack of a specific Dutch quality derives from our national character, says Wermuth. "We are not proud of the fact that we're Dutch, and we don't know what is specific about us."

Dutch entertainers competing on the international market with the Americans and the British have one very big handicap: language. "Anouk is enormously talented, but you can't say that about the writing of her lyrics." And then there's pronunciation. "The Dutch think they're good at it, but a lot of our artists don't have an easy familiarity with the language." Wermuth does, however, see opportunities here in the long run. Since more and more English is being used in Dutch schools, the general level will rise. This does not mean that a Dutch horde is about to conquer the American market.
"If Ali B were suddenly to rap in English, it would sound acceptable to our ears, but not to the American audiences. He'll never be asked to do a masterclass in the States. He just doesn't have the quality."
Entertainers will speak better English in the future thanks to lessons at the Dutch pop and rock academies and by schooling from the record companies. The commercial music industry recognises the value of brush-up courses. Wermuth: "Ilse Delange has clearly been working on her English. You hear it in her lyrics."
One of the reasons for Tiësto's popularity could well be the absence of speech or lyrics. "It's only an idea," says Wermuth cautiously, "but maybe we're prominent in dance-music precisely because there's no language in it." The same might go for Jan Akkerman. His guitar playing, without lyrics, is highly regarded internationally.
Dutch pop music is a sector in which commerce and government support exist side by side, says Wermuth. Both parties make a case for promoting Nederpop internationally; both industry and the government examine the commercial potential of individual tracks. But promoting Dutch culture has nothing to do with any of that; Dutch pop music's lack of individual character makes it difficult to predict if a band could score a foreign hit. "I can't judge it," admits Wermuth. "It's trial and error. Shooting at the sky." It's just as hard for policy makers as it is for the marketing execs. So promoting a Dutch group happens only instinctively.
In hindsight we can see why BZN succeeded in odd countries like Indonesia and Malaysia without any government help. "They like BZN's sweet melody line out there." Elaborating on that sort of approach, the idea arose recently that maybe the Dutch

Gothic band Within Temptation could catch on in Germany. "Their music is a sort of modern Wagner, doing covers of Kate Bush among others." The promotion was farmed out to MusicXport.nl, a musical version of the Instituut Néerlandais, in which the Stichting Conamus, the government subsidised Dutch Rock & Pop Institute and the record industry work together. And it hit the mark; Within Temptation was a hit in Germany.

If Dutch pop music is going to make an impression abroad then there will have to be more offices like MusicXport.nl, says Wermuth. Success can also come through an active deployment of new Dutch cultural attachés in foreign countries. "The present generation were almost fond of The Beatles, but thought The Rolling Stones too noisy. The coming generation of attachés, however, grew up with a diversity of pop music. They're much more likely to request a cultural programme with pop music." The Nits – a band that many cultural policy makers see as representing high culture – is already a requested guest act at foreign state occasions.

Cultural attachés usually look for a mixture of established and younger entertainers, says Wermuth who, as a member of the board of the Dutch Rock & Pop Institute, is closely involved in the final choice of entertainers. Such a selection takes into account the extent to which the musician can click with entertainers from the country he is due to visit. "It wouldn't be such a good idea to send a white punk band to the slum neighbourhoods in South Africa. But if you let black, Dutch-speaking hiphoppers go, then that might lead to something. They could seek contact with black South African hiphoppers. That the Dutch are rapping in the language of the former oppressors might result in interesting culture clashes. The same goes for the group Zuco 103 with its Brazilian singer Lilian Vieira. If such a band is in Brazil then they might succeed in getting a foot in the door."

Marco Borsato, DJ Tiësto and 2 Unlimited attained their national and international star status to all intents and purposes without large amounts of government subsidy, but that does not mean that the government completely ignores pop culture. For somewhat less famous groups like Bettie Serveert or The Sheer it is difficult to survive in the Netherlands, or beyond, says Wermuth. The same goes for a lot of local black music groups which, without support, are confined to performing within their own ethnic communities.

Unlike theatre or classical music, subsidies don't go to companies and orchestras, but to pop venues and festivals, which can then use that money to pay the performing artist. There is also government support, but to a lesser extent, for Dutch artists performing abroad. They can receive a contribution to their travel and accommodation expenses, called tour support. Bigger artists who are promoted abroad by their record label no longer receive subsidy, but they are few. Wermuth notes that artists are increasingly applying for tour support, chasing up the noticeable demand in Eastern Europe. Strangely enough, it is unknown how many Dutch artists perform abroad per year. "It is largely a do-it-yourself sector," is how Wermuth explains the absence of statistics. "Till now a lot goes out of sight, but the commercial and subsidised parties in the market are starting to make it their business to cash in on the increasing demand."

Sandra Jongenelen is a freelance journalist for *Het Financieele Dagblad* and *Kunstbeeld*, and a member of the advisory council for *Boekman*, a journal for art, culture and policy.

Close the Gap Between Art and Commerce

1994: De Digitale Stad (The Digital City) is inaugurated in Amsterdam, one of the first cities in the world to offer its citizens the possibility of experiencing the virtual world.

2004: The eight o'clock news announces the festive launching of *Killzone*, the first Dutch PlayStation game, produced by the Dutch company Gorilla.

Anyone who concludes from this product launch that the Netherlands is at the forefront of the new media has been asleep for the past few years, or hasn't been into a toy shop. Back in 2001, the games industry's revenue had already surpassed that of the film industry. Games generate an annual turnover of around $24 billion, whereas films only bring in $21 billion. Why has this development largely passed the Netherlands by?

It's not as if nothing has happened in Dutch digital culture since 1994. In the tradition of De Digitale Stad, the VPRO, and V2, a flourishing culture of autonomous interactive productions has grown up over the past decade. Individuals and cultural organizations have developed many innovative research projects, social applications and digital art projects. Arts foundations were quick to see the potential of the new media and are now supporting such projects with subsidies. The new media in the Netherlands have primarily developed within the domain of the experimental and the artistic. This is very valuable, but over the past decade we have seen digital media comprising more than interactive experiments alone. Although that television newscast presented the first Dutch PlayStation game as a breakthrough, in other countries a broad range of new media applications has been available for years: videogames on CD-rom, PlayStation games, Internet on cell phones, interactive television channels and programs, blogs and online communities.
And these are certainly not all made in America or Japan. The British game designer Peter Molyneux created a series of videogames whose Scorsese-like atmosphere made authorship an established concept in the world of games. In France, the small animation studio Chman created the virtual world of Banja on the Internet, which turned out to be so successful that it has been translated into six languages and led to a television series. There is even a Banja movie in the works. What makes these products exceptional is that they have had huge international influence on the new media industry and on our ideas about what new media can do. Peter Molyneux's company was bought up years ago by an American games conglomerate, just as Hollywood has always scooped up European filmmakers. In a similar way to the film industry, European new media makers have proven capable of coming up with innovative, high-quality productions that are then imitated by the rest of the world. In ten years the field of new media has become very broad and diverse: from commercial blockbusters to interactive installations in museums, from online journalistic productions and magazines to photologs and Friendster.
It would seem that precisely because we Dutch were so far ahead of the rest of the world in the mid-nineties we never considered adjusting our perspective on the new media. We have a fixed idea of what these are. The dialectics of progress appear to have proven

correct here. All sorts of new-media institutions popped up in the Netherlands, and the government reacted with effective subsidy regulations to enable these non-commercial initiatives to mature. Simultaneously, during the nineties, there emerged the great promise of the new economy and the Internet. Everything that was not artistic, the Dutch thought, could be realised within the commercial domain.

This created an ostensible chasm between the commercial world and the arts. The middle ground did not exist, and in fact still does not exist in the Netherlands. Before the so-called *e-conomy* could come to full bloom in this country, the new rage turned out to be no more than a soap bubble. After the stock market crash, the new media were suddenly regarded with scepticism: it had all been a false dream; nobody would take the slightest interest in interactive proceedings. After all, wasn't television far more comfortable? The Internet would never be more than a glorified teletext or a promotional brochure for the traditional media.

And looking at it from a Dutch perspective, this was probably true. PCM abandoned all its Internet activities, MagicMinds went bankrupt, public broadcasters concentrated as hard as possible on internal policies and the popularity of Beta studies proved short-lived. While the Netherlands dozed off, the new media industry in other countries got back on its feet. Having laid aside their megalomaniac expectations, new companies and government programs now arose that viewed the new media in a more realistic light: no longer the *promise* of a New World, they are simply *part* of our world. In France, the CNC film fund has broadened its horizons by providing subsidy and investment measures for the creation of videogames, DVDs and artistic digital productions. The English program Nesta stimulates close collaboration between arts and sciences by awarding grants for cultural/scientific projects within the broad scope of the creative industry. The British public broadcasting company BBC and the commercial broadcasting company Sky are world leaders in the field of interactive television. With the help of government investment, Luxembourg has developed a flourishing industry in special effects and digital animation.

At the same time, and almost unnoticed, the public's use of the new media has increased tremendously. Over 65% of the Dutch population now goes online. Recent American research shows that young people spend an average of 16 hours a week on the Internet (not counting e-mail); in the Netherlands this is about 7 hours. Internet usage is still increasing, while television viewing is declining. Moreover, young people consider the Internet to be a more trustworthy medium than the press. The digital media are no longer avant garde; instead they have become part of everyone's world. The Dutch new-media infrastructure should therefore not only focus on the small audiences that faithfully attend the World Wide Video Festival and the Deaf Festival every year, but become just as varied as the media themselves.

With a steadily growing proportion of media consumption comprising games, the Internet and other digital media, do we want the Dutch public to consume only foreign entertainment and culture? Must Dutch youths be left with only American games to play, or is it important to produce Dutch cultural items in the digital age too? If we leave it to the commercial sector, there's a good chance we will end up with anaemic copies of American genre games. A broad middle ground exists between the experiments of the art world and games that are made only for financial gain. The new media can be better understood by comparing them with film than with the arts, because film also covers the broad spectrum from abstract animation to documentary, artistic drama and commercial blockbuster. If we want to ensure that the Dutch produce games that have the thematic ambition of films like *Simon*, or the aesthetic innovation of directors like Johan van der Keuken or Fow Pyng Hu, we will have to take action.

Artistically inclined Dutch game makers can close the gap between autonomous art and commerce by looking further than the small in-crowd of the art world and focusing on a broader audience. And commercial producers can do the same thing by providing content that is truly distinctive in the international market.
Every mode of expression requires its own criteria for the measurement of quality and prediction of artistic or commercial potential. Each type also requires its own financing scheme. This is as true for small- and large-scale artistic productions as it is for ambitious video games. New-media productions cannot be created on the same budget as an art installation or a web site. Producing a game costs just as much as making a feature film, or even more. The arts foundations do their best to periodically grant money for the creation of an unusual game, even though their budgets, being intended for small-scale autonomous new media, barely allow them to do this. Much better suited for this purpose would be investment measures based on an integrated policy by the Department of Economic Affairs, the Ministry of Education, Cultural Affairs and Science, and the Department of Finance. Such a policy would have to focus on stimulating high-quality productions in all areas in order to create a multifaceted new-media industry. And these applications need not only be aimed at the Dutch market. Because if Dutch people can play American games, isn't the reverse also true? Dutch design, documentaries and television formats are just a few examples of successful Dutch cultural exports. The new media are particularly suited to the international cultural market - and this includes Dutch new media. It is a lot simpler to translate an animated video game into another language than it is to subtitle Dutch drama for a foreign audience. Moreover, reaching an international audience is easy, because the new media can be dispersed through new digital distribution channels. The Dutch Internet channel *Submarinechannel*, for example, has a worldwide audience that is only 25% Dutch. A new generation of media consumers will be accustomed to making its own selection of programs and channels from all over the world. The new media offer a great opportunity to small nations that want to become international players.

Femke Wolting is director and co-owner of Submarine, which produces documentaries, films and interactive media projects, and the founder of the Internet channel Submarinechannel, which produces and distributes new-media products. She also directs documentaries.

New Dutch Design: From the Inside Out

"How, in what form, and why should the Netherlands introduce its new design to the outside world?" For me the image conjures up two different images of the Netherlands, one circumscribed by arrows pointing outwards and the other by arrows aiming inwards, pointing to ourselves.

The spread of arrows pointing outwards was my first reaction. That is, how do we currently work? How are we now making ourselves known abroad? We do it through exhibitions and events in all the interesting countries of the world, and in fine English-language publications. But I also realised right away that this image is not going to help us further – it is a dead end. It is not able to lead us to new insights because it will continue to be about the outside, not the inside. The configuration of arrows pointing into the Netherlands springs from my second reaction. In what form should we bring new Dutch design to the outside world in the coming years – and why? These questions are much more exciting to contemplate because they compel us to take a very close look at the story that the Netherlands has to tell in other countries.

The cultural strength of Dutch design
—

The Netherlands is noted for design of the artistic sort, and is an undisputed leader in the international conceptual avant garde. The high quality of Dutch design and the recognition it has received worldwide are the result of years of effort by a select group of exceptionally talented designers, by a variety of initiatives, of which Droog is the most important, by the media, by educational institutions, and by cultural organizations like the Mondriaan Foundation and the Premsela Foundation. It is a splendid achievement – and one that should certainly give us pause.

But maybe it is all a bit overblown. After all, the cult popularity of Dutch design is still founded on a small number of conceptually very interesting products. The cultural impact is great but it springs from a very narrow base. Can we expand that base and if so, how? Should we expand with an eye to increasing economic value as well? At the moment, the economic value of Dutch design is minimal. We are saddled with the unpleasant paradox of being very good in design but not very good at profiting from it.

We are now faced with the challenge of thinking up a next step. It is tempting to begin with the things that are missing in the current situation and then indicate what has to be changed. People will be quick to call for more bridge-building between the world of Dutch design and the business sector. Invariably, they will add that they are convinced that the design world has to be professionalised – in its business aspects, of course. To my way of thinking, this is a trap. Sometimes it is better to leave things as they are, so as not to take the shine off success. Dutch design is an enormous achievement, one from which we can certainly still profit. But let us not violate that success, based as it is on exceptional cultural quality, by forcing it into an economic straitjacket. Dutch design is a uniquely strong, conceptual cultural statement. It must not be treated as a cash cow. To do so is to negate everything Dutch design stands for.

We must once again spread our wings. The fine reputation of Dutch design certainly provides us with a good point of departure but at the moment, it does not tell us how we should proceed. However, if we begin to feel we are in over our heads, we can be assured that that typically Dutch, cocksure, curious, flexible, innovative and pragmatic spirit will come to our rescue and provide us with very good solutions.

The new product is a process
—

What then will be the new directions for Dutch design?
Having been through a period in which thinking in terms of solutions has been the guiding principle, we have now reached a point where processes are more important. It cannot be otherwise because the questions being asked are complex and no longer satisfied by one-dimensional answers. Ideologies or strategies that can unequivocally show us the way in shaping the world no longer exist. This is true not only in the social and economic arenas but in the cultural as well.

We have to look at the border areas between diverse perspectives, in our approach to a problem. In my view, design will play an important role in the finding and framing of solutions in these areas. We must work together more than ever before. At the same time, we have really very little experience with co-operative efforts. This is certainly true in the case of today's 'networked' phrasing of questions. In this kind of questioning, the desired result is not yet known and a complex process must be gone through in order to find the solution.

There is an urgent need for new processes that will allow multidisciplinary Cupertino to bear fruit, a collaboration that is not based on compromise by the dissolving of differences but rather one that provides the space for discovering an added value that the participating parties could not have achieved separately. A new version of the old consensus model?

New Dutch design: share the differences
—

I am defending here the qualities of that quintessentially Dutch consensus model but in the same breath suggesting that it be reinvented. The new model will have one very major difference. In the eyes of many, the old model led to 'second best' solutions because everybody had to agree at least in part with the outcome. In the process, the controversial aspects of problems were lost and the problems themselves disappeared from view, resulting in supposed solutions in which the real problems were left unaddressed.
I am arguing for a new consensus model in which the guiding principle is not the levelling of differences but rather the sharing of differences. We are entering a period in which we are going to discover the fantastic potential that the power and added value created by the forming of coalitions and alliances has for the badly needed renewal of our culture. And I for one am fascinated by what design can do in that process.

Worldwide, the idea is emerging that creativity is important in the development of our society and, as a result, more consideration is being given to creative processes. It is noteworthy that the economic sector is also getting involved. Co-operation between different parties, crossovers between sectors and disciplines and the creation of unexpected solutions in the design process are receiving a lot of attention.

Designers have very good credentials for functioning in such complex contexts because from early on, they are trained to work on 'networked' propositions. A designer works in a multidimensional, sometimes paradoxical mix of analysis, inspiration, expertise, rationale and intuition, simultaneously and continually moving step by step towards a final result. Design is one of the professions in which lateral and creative thinking is embedded in a solution-oriented work process.

Expand the frontiers: from the inside out
—

Introducing design to complex problem areas that would normally fall outside the range of 'the designer' is certainly one of the Netherlands' bigger success stories. And the trend is growing. More and more people are organising multidisciplinary creative collaborations. In platforms, clubs and networks, often with an international character, creativity and business are being brought together in a single context, based on productive and constructive mutual involvement.

Thus I think that there has to be a design policy in which purposeful space is created for investing in and developing these ideas. Opportunities for international co-operation must allow for the strengths we have been describing to be stimulated further and developed in depth. A basic condition of this is that the systems of support for policy in the cultural, social and economic sectors have to be hauled out of their isolation and made to work together.

The Netherlands has substantial qualities that enable it to do this. We have to accept the challenge to again take the lead and demonstrate what can be achieved by this new way of thinking. Because that's where our great inner strength lies: in innovative thinking – and innovative doing.

Peik Suyling, an artist and designer, directs the Young Designers & Industry Foundation and teaches at the Design Lab of the Gerrit Rietveld Academy. He is also director of the Open Amsterdam Society, a network for innovative relationships. "I try to create quests where people, including myself, are challenged to clear new paths."

"Thank God My Name Doesn't Sound Dutch"

Sydney Neter, Barbara Truyen, Wouter Barendrecht interviewed by *Hans Beerekamp*

Film sales agents are called *filmverkopers* in the Netherlands. Anybody wishing
to market Dutch cultural products abroad had better know as much about business
and economics as they know about their cultural product. Claudia Landsberger, of
the promotional organization Holland Film, selected three prominent Dutch film sales
agents to give me their views about the market position of Dutch celluloid abroad:
Sydney Neter of SND Films, Wouter Barendrecht of Fortissimo Film Sales, and Jan
Röfekamp of Films Transit International. As Jan Röfekamp operates from Montreal his
interests are represented in Holland by Barbara Truyen. I spoke with her, Sydney Neter,
and Wouter Barendrecht.

Sydney Neter

—

SND Films is Sydney Neter's one-man operation on the Leidsestraat in Amsterdam.
He specialises in short films and documentaries and has more than 200 titles on his
catalogue to which he adds as many as 25 new titles each year. A third of the short
films, mostly animations, and two thirds of the documentaries, are Dutch. Ninety per
cent of all his sales are to television broadcasters. His sales to DVD outlets are growing
comfortably. Neter has a turnover of about 200,000 euros per annum, of which 25-30
per cent is his commission. The Dutch Oscar-winning animation film *Father and Daughter*
by Michael Dudok de Wit remains SND's biggest seller, with returns of almost 50,000
euros. The film cost four times that amount, the remainder being covered by subsidies
and broadcast companies.

Neter can make a reasonable living from his business, but he has to work hard. Most
of his films are funded by subsidies. Most of his showings are at festivals, which while
they do not pay in themselves, are calling cards that can lead to wider sales. Only some
gay and lesbian festivals in North America have real money to spend says Neter, and
they pay only 200 euros, covering administration costs. "You don't ask for money from
the A-festivals, like Cannes, Toronto, Berlin, Rotterdam."

According to Neter, film directors and producers should not pay too much attention to
their intended market: "In the end, you simply have to make the films you want to make!"

When asked about how enterprising Dutch film producers are, Neter says: "Producers
here don't want to take any risks. They only go into production when 95% of the costs
have been met by subsidies and the TV companies." Neter himself is not a producer,
"but it may yet have to come to that."

As a permanent member of the advisory committee for short films of the Film Fund
Neter is involved in deciding which short films will get made in Holland. He pays more
attention to the artistic quality of the submitted scripts and likely interest of the Dutch
public than to international potential. There may well be major opportunities abroad for
Dutch documentaries on homosexual subjects, for example, but as there is little call

for further emancipation in Holland such films are hardly ever made any more. What Holland really lacks, according to Neter, are light documentaries to compare with his own American hit *Tupperware*, but he readily admits that many American documentaries are more superficial than their Dutch counterparts. Even political documentaries like *Fahrenheit 9/11* and *Supersize Me* amount to little more than pamphlets.

In fact, Neter uses his foreign films as work horses to pull his Dutch films along. "Do people see me as a Dutch sales agent? No. Thank goodness my name doesn't sound particularly Dutch. I could advertise myself as a Dutchman, but I think it would be more of a handicap than an advantage. NPB Sales, who handle most of the Dutch television productions, has acquired a bit of a reputation for its unsaleable films. Although Dutch documentaries do have a good reputation, there simply aren't enough quality products for the market abroad."

Barbara Truyen

—

Jan Röfekamp, once one of the founders of the politically engaged distribution house Fugitive Cinema in Amsterdam, left for Canada in the eighties. There he started Films Transit International, now by far the most prominent sales company specialising in documentaries in the world. According to Amsterdam Branch Manager Barbara Truyen, there are nine Dutch titles in their recently revised catalogue, about ten per cent of the total. Doing best at the moment is John Appel's *The Last Victory*, about the Palio horse race in Siena. Truyen is especially proud of the sale of British theatrical rights: "It's the first time in living memory that a Dutch documentary has appeared on the big screen in England." Films Transit International does by far the most of its business with TV broadcasters. Their turnover is bigger than that of SND Films, but smaller than Fortissimo Film Sales.

The somewhat older documentary by Jaap van Hoewijk, *Procedure 769* about the death sentence in America is also still doing well. In the past, Marijke Jongbloed's series *Fatal Reaction* about the limited marriage prospects of highly educated women in places such as Moscow and Bombay, and Jos de Putter's Chechen epos *The Making of a New Empire* got some good results. Experience would seem to indicate that documentaries with non-Dutch subjects sell best. This rule does not apply to feature films, nor to anything by Alex van Warmerdam, or to children's films.

Truyen: "Clients don't ask me: 'Have you got another Dutch documentary?' It doesn't actually matter much to them where a film comes from, as long as it's good."

She feels some countries, such as Canada and Australia, are good at promoting their own films. And the French hold a *rencontre* (meeting) for their documentaries in the US, which works better than exhibiting at the big festivals where there are so many filmmakers present at the same time that they lose each other in the crowd: "It's often the case that good things come in small packages. Promotion isn't all about money, it's more about know-how and who you know. By organizing special lunches for distributors, independently of the festivals, you make your contacts more formal and less noncommittal. You're then investing in the experience of the participating producers and directors too." According to Barbara Truyen, there are too many producers, though that isn't specifically a Dutch problem. What is certainly lacking are producers who are neither up-tight nor spoilt: "If you're really passionate, the film will get made! Americans don't get subsidies, so you see more drive there."

The Dutch welfare state obstructs the making of really political films, films which fight injustice: "The culture of looking the other way is very Dutch, and fatal to the making of documentaries with a sense of urgency."

Wouter Barendrecht

—

Fortissimo Film Sales, with its headquarters in Amsterdam and a branch in Hong Kong, where founder and co-chairman Wouter Barendrecht lives, is one of the most important sales companies for directors' movies from Asia, North America and Australia as well as Europe. Barendrecht started his career in film by working for the festivals in Berlin, Utrecht and Rotterdam and began to build up a worldwide cinephile network. Among the many directors in his stable are Wong Kar-wai, Jim Jarmusch, Peter Greenaway and Alex van Warmerdam. All the stars from the Far East are as good as family to him and his name is pronounced in many different ways. His nickname is 'reverse banana: white on the outside, yellow on the inside'.

Fortissimo's annual turnover amounts to about 15 million euros. A small but growing proportion of the films are documentaries. Less than ten per cent of the titles and the turnover involve Dutch films. Barendrecht has achieved success with *De jurk* (The Dress) and *Kleine Teun* (Little Tony), and with Pieter Kramer's high-camp musical *Ja zuster, nee zuster* (Yes Nurse, No Nurse), which Fortissimo not only got into the competition at Berlin, but made a hit with Japanese teenage girls and at gay festivals all over the world.

Barendrecht: "Dutch films are a difficult product to sell. I'm very enthusiastic about the co-operation I've had from the Dutch consulates and particularly from Holland Film, both with regard to information exchange as well as concrete, practical matters. It may sound meaningless, but sending a load of Sister Klivia dresses for the première in Kuala Lumpur can be of crucial importance to a local distributor."

For Loes Luca's fans in Hong Kong and San Francisco, it's not particularly important that she's Dutch, but it does matter that she seems a bit weird and exotic: "Films specifically rooted in a particular culture often seem to do best. Look at François Ozon, Takeshi Kitano, Pedro Almodóvar, Wong Kar-wai. But if you market a film as a director's movie, as we usually do, it doesn't matter very much which country it's set in, because it's Warmerdam-land, or Kitano-country. Almodóvar isn't good because he's Spanish, but because he's Almodóvar."

To build up such an author/director's reputation involves a long road through all the international film festivals: "Developing talent is the most important thing. You have to create freedom for a film-maker, first by allowing him to leave a calling card, in the form of short films or low-budget films, for example. In Europe, these are financed with 'soft money', meaning subsidies. In North America, it's money from a credit card borrowed from grandma. In Asia, they often earn the initial investment by making commercials. This is especially true in up-and-coming film cultures such as Thailand and Argentina."

Although Holland still has a well-functioning subsidy system, politics seems a relatively long way off: "In comparison with France, Italy, the US or Thailand, the film industry's political lobby is insignificant here. Music and dance seem to manage much better."

Barendrecht also wonders if there are still prospects for the growth of Dutch co-productions, and if Dutch connections with the international circuit aren't in danger of being lost altogether: "Hardly any directors finance their films entirely or even mainly in their own countries. Financing is almost always worldwide, on the basis of the recognized qualities of previous work. Scripts are relatively unimportant. Wong Kar-wai never writes scripts. Walter Salles in Brazil, Lucrecia Martel in Argentina, Almodóvar in Spain, all of them get international financing. Taiwan, which has about the same population as Holland, shows Hollywood block-busters 99% of the time, but has three of the most renowned film authors on the film festival circuit: Tsai Ming-liang, Hou Hsiao-hsien and Edward Yang. When Edward Yang recently wanted to show his film *Yi Yi* in Taipei, he had to rent a cinema to show it to his friends."

In spite of the relatively comfortable subsidy system, the position of Dutch film in the international network is weak. Barendrecht offers two possible explanations: "In the first place, talent is not democratically distributed and can only be developed to a limited extent. In the second place, there's something missing in the attitude of producers here. They often lack passion for their own films and a sense of urgency. If an application for funding is refused, they often content themselves with nothing. Grant money should be less democratically distributed. You have to help real talent get through the making of a second film. After a strong debut, the second film is generally problematic, and you can only really expect results from the third. But if you keep wanting to crumble the cookie evenly, a talented film-maker may have to wait for years to make his second, let alone his third film.

"It's also important that directors keep the exploitation rights for their older films. That way, someone like Jim Jarmusch can keep his head above water. Dutch producers need to travel more too, to look for creative solutions. You see them at Cannes or Toronto, but never at the American Film Market in Los Angeles, where the real business gets done. They should also consider study trips to London, to the Royal Bank of Scotland, which is very involved in financing film and couldn't care less whether your project is going to be made in English. It can be made in German or Cantonese as far as they're concerned!"

Hans Beerekamp was the film editor of *NRC Handelsblad* from 1979 to 2003. Since September 1, 2003, he has written a daily television review for that paper. He is also a permanent guest lecturer in film criticism at the University of Groningen.

International
Mediation

No Interior Without Exterior

Peter Hewitt, CEO of the Arts Council of England, is at present travelling the world
on a four-month sabbatical, visiting a string of countries to investigate how things are
done elsewhere. When I met him recently in Holland it became clear to me once again
how important it is not only to travel, but to receive guests. Travelling is an investment,
but so is hospitality and being a host. I hope Hewitt was inspired during his visit to
Holland, because meeting him certainly inspired me to take a fresh look at a number
of issues.

The Arts Council of England works in a fundamentally different way to the Dutch
cultural funding bodies. The practices of the Arts Council offer a number of illuminating
perspectives on the functioning of funding bodies, perspectives which may well be
relevant to the Mondriaan Foundation. It was particularly the differences which set me
thinking about improving some of the practices of the Mondriaan Foundation, though
the similarities are important too.

International Mediation has never been so urgent. We live in paradoxical times. Recently,
there has been a rising hubbub of voices declaring that Dutch art is beginning to lose its
connection with international culture. The Dutch art sector is accused of provincialism.
At the same time, we are increasingly oriented towards self-examination. The theme
of this year's Book Week was Dutch national history and the debate about a museum
of Dutch national history has been revived. At the moment, a super-advisory council is
conferring to discuss the formulation of 'standards of knowledge' in education. These
standards will include valuable aspects of Dutch culture and history, which will be
disseminated to students as part of their education. The body of knowledge, with its
highlights of national history, will be an expression of our Dutch identity.

One important question is asked only half-heartedly: just how nationally do we
want to set these standards of history and culture? How Dutch or un-Dutch are our
icons allowed to be, to quote Bas Heijne elsewhere in this publication? What should
we teach young people about the international character of Holland? What perspective
do we have to offer them with regard to the role and place of Holland in the world?
The Netherlands has always been a trading nation with open borders, a country of
mariners and adventurers. This is an important part of our identity. Our history is a part
of European society and of the world community. "It is the contrast with other cultures
and ways of thinking that gives colour to our own identity, enabling us both to spotlight
it and to put it in context." according to educationalist Henk Wagenaar, writing about
the standards of history and culture in the *Volkskrant* of 20th January 2005.

The focus on a national perspective, by both liberal and socialist parties, not only
denies young people the opportunity of giving meaning to Holland in the world, but
is also reminiscent of the attempts of the European nation states in the 19th century
to use national history to promote national unity. History has taught us that a lack
of mediation, combined with an overweening urge to formulate an identity, can have

major consequences. In an era of globalization and far-reaching European cooperation, it is a challenge to give shape to our own identity in an intelligent manner. Thomas Michelon gives us an international perspective on this discussion in this publication. The changeability of the international arena makes it a difficult task for all the Western European countries to formulate government policy in this area. Michelon thinks Western Europe as a whole should be subjected to a critical, independent review.

I agree with him. What goes for Europe certainly goes for Holland. We pay too much attention to ourselves. It could well be that the key solution of our problems will only become visible when we learn to look at ourselves through the eyes of an outsider. Then it won't just be a case of admitting un-Dutch elements into the 'standards of knowledge', or encouraging travel abroad. It will be a case of true participation in the international (professional) community. Artistic quality is valued in the international context. It is in this context that it is decided which art or artist is relevant to current developments at a given moment. International appraisal is important feedback on any cultural impulse from within the Netherlands. That is why it is crucial that our connection with the international podium is maintained, even stimulated.

International awareness of the art world is inseparably linked to curiosity. Participation in international networks, getting to know and showing international art are ways of strengthening international relationships. Artists, professionals and of course the public, need to be able to form an image of what's going on elsewhere. Only in this way can Dutch developments be placed in a global framework. This isn't a question of incidental projects, but of a permanent dialogue with artists and organizations from elsewhere. The idea of Holland as a free port, as an international meeting place is crucial.

Maria Hlavajova and Ann Demeester teach us a lesson in their contribution in these pages. International activities in Holland will take on meaning when they have a greater range than "a practice produced around a hypothetical understanding of the international reality, and reproducing the coordinates of an international arena in a small-scale, model format, in the safe proximity to home waters." The free port policy is only effective when it no longer breathes the atmosphere of a test run. Foreign guest curators, theatre-makers and other artistic professionals can only function when their visit is no longer noncommittal and neutral, when the host is open to feedback, demonstrably interested in what the other has to say and convinced of the value of the contribution being made to the (Dutch) art world.

The Dutch art world does not shine either in curiosity or in openness to feedback. Indeed, we feel that giving criticism, as Johan Simons says in this publication, is 'not being fair to our colleagues'. This is why the debate around each other's work is always a slow starter. Nor do we take much notice of the opinions of outsiders unfamiliar with Dutch habits of thought. This comes from over-estimating our own worth. This is not strictly a Dutch phenomenon, by the way: the average person overestimates the value of his own work by around 75 per cent. Statistically, the functioning of half of all people (including museum directors, theatre-makers and artists) must score below 50%. But that's how we deal with the frightening reality of our own ignorance.

"There is so much fear and so little curiosity," says Alida Neslo in this publication.

She hits the nail on the head. International mediation is necessary to the arts and for society as a whole. We can turn it to our advantage only when we go into the world with an open heart and look around. Do it!

Gitta Luiten has been the director of the Mondriaan Foundation, funding body for the promotion of the visual arts, design and cultural heritage of the Netherlands since 2001. Earlier she was political advisor to the State Secretary for Culture and Media, Rick van der Ploeg, spokeswoman for the Council for Culture and has worked for the Rijksmuseum.

'Visionary Netherlands'
Notes on the Dutch International Paradox

"The Netherlands has long had a world role out of proportion to its size,"[1] *The Economist* stated in a very informative, detailed study in 2002 providing both historical and contemporary insights into a number of specifically Dutch phenomena of recent social, economic, and political developments in the country. The survey provides an impressive account of the accomplishments of the Dutch, often the result of using internationally unknown or unprecedented tactics, methods, and policies. At the same time, however, throughout the text, Dutch achievements are undermined by references to some sort of a crisis – a current 'disillusion,' 'considerable dissatisfaction,' or 'uncertainty,' as if these were prevailing sentiments in the Netherlands. It is hard to determine whether these feelings have to do with the unwillingness of the Dutch to imagine themselves differently, whether they are nostalgic for a position the country had in the past but has lost, or whether there is a realization that such a standing cannot be maintained in today's world. Although the authors state with a wink that 'the Dutch are famous for complaining', it is clear that despite (or because) of decades of success and prosperity, the Netherlands has arrived at a point where it has to reformulate itself vis-à-vis the new challenges international developments present. In art no less than in politics.

One could ask whether a current discussion in the Netherlands that evolved around the loosely formulated question, 'Has Dutch art lost its international reputation?' might belong to this process of reformulation. Disguised as a longing for the past, this kind of discussion is no substitute for a profound analysis of real problems the Dutch contemporary art scene needs to engage. Might it be, for example, contrary to popular opinion on this issue, that the Netherlands actually does have an 'international story', but lacks its own narrative, which, paradoxically, disqualifies it in the international arena?

In winter 2004 the Brussels institution Bozar announced the grand opening of the jubilee show *Visionary Belgium*, a multifaceted lavish exhibition conceived by the late Harald Szeemann with the intention of 'capturing the spirit of a country', following exhibitions with a similar intention in Switzerland in 1991 and Austria in 1996. Indirectly, this transdisciplinary presentation celebrating the special features of Belgian history and culture created a great commotion in Dutch art circles. The Swiss curator, who sadly passed away before his *piece de resistance* opened to the general public, proclaimed that this kind of show, one that illustrated the idiosyncrasies and particularities of a certain national artistic tradition, would not be possible in countries such as Germany and France. The 'Sinbad of the art world', the pet name often attributed to him by the German press, believed that only four European countries were sufficiently non-conformist and peculiar, deviant and extravagant, to be considered visionary, namely Switzerland, Austria, Belgium, and Poland. In the Netherlands this issue was taken personally and the question arose of whether Szeemann, despite the above-mentioned claim, would ever consider compiling a massive retrospective exhibition on Dutch culture. The answer was a simple and straightforward: "No."

The general feeling seemed to be that the Dutch art scene is no lomger relevant on a global scale. This only sharpened a suspicion, repeatedly and carefully articulated amongst cultural practitioners, that the Netherlands used to be avant-garde but had now lost its position as a forerunner of new trends and emerging developments in the visual arts. Such a statement is of course impossible to prove, especially as in the field of art we tend not to look at facts and figures, at graphs and statistics.
Do foreign curators pay fewer visits to the Netherlands than they did in the seventies and eighties? Are Dutch artists underrepresented in biennials and large-scale shows abroad? Are Dutch institutions no longer considered to be forward thinking in matters of contemporary art practice? These may indeed need to remain rhetorical questions.

Being 'visionary' mostly implies that there is a sensation of walking on the edge, of undertaking certain risks to test innovative ideas, thoughts, concepts, and modes of implementing them that are potentially dangerous, potentially wrong, and potentially unacceptable. It might be that such risks are not extremely likely to be taken within the Dutch context, where practical instinct dominates over vision, and where vigilantly calculated actions are chosen above bold, impulsive decisions, pragmatic utopianism is preferred over blind idealism, strategy and organised exchange above spontaneous reactions and organic dialogue, and systems and rules, strict patterns are esteemed higher than creative, potentially useful disobedience, which administered in moderate portions might bring incredible results.

In *Visionary Belgium*, Szeemann himself indirectly addressed where a sensitive development of a vision might lead if overtaken by extensive attention to systematization and ordering. The exhibit includes a section on a remarkable pair of thinkers called Otlet and La Fontaine. In 1895, the Belgian bibliographer, entrepreneur, and pacifist Paul Otlet and his close friend and collaborator senator Henri La Fontaine established the *Repertoire Bibliographique Universel (RBU)*, an ambitious attempt at developing a master bibliography of all human knowledge, a forefather of the World Wide Web, comprising over twelve million individual index cards and documents, as well as the categorisation system behind it. Together with the *Union of International Associations* they co-founded in 1910, which involved international reference materials on 'international associations', the *RBU* stemmed from the desire to create an enormous and ever-expanding network of international exchange. Although they had a grand vision of what the world might become (a place of universal peace and harmony), the main focus was on obsessively setting up categorisation systems and organisational structures, which would create more clarity and facilitate different forms of global interaction. The system they developed did not take into account that both vision and creativity often refuse objective classification and clear-cut, straightforward solutions. That very dogma of systems and categories, definitions and control, was in the end fatal to the dream.

Without a doubt, the Dutch inclination to organize and structure has created a distinctive, politically correct model of the field of art in which we operate today.
The system, unlike its contents – to draw on Szeemann again – is usually greatly admired as a prototype for novel cultural policy; some foreign, institutional, and legislative structures are even modelled after the arrangement we are now complaining about.
The organization of artistic life in the Netherlands is competently embedded in the

principles of decentralization, inclusiveness, and consensus. The generosity visible in public subsidies for art and culture in the Netherlands certainly should be applauded and maintained; however, the results call for serious repositioning. It is an oft-repeated argument that we feel needs to be reiterated here: the system concentrates on quality and ensures a wide range of diverse positions rather than recognizing their essential quality, which is usually associated with a more selective model that supports fewer, high quality manifestations (and with larger amounts allowing for concentrated work at a different level of significance). A similar point could be made about the principle of consensus: from an organizational perspective the notion evokes the virtues of democracy, but in art this model simply prefers good to better. And however strange it might sound to point out the destructive nature of the system's inclusiveness, internally, the fragmented structure of the Dutch art world simply lacks the energy unleashed by being refused or turned away, precisely the kind of energy that could potentially nurture a productive change.

Could it be that the complaint about Dutch disconnection from internationaldevelopments results from a similar tendency to prescribe and control, and has evolved horizontally around the notions of inclusiveness and consensus? Could it have happened in the way described in the following possibly fictional scenario?

The powerful political instruments of sanctuary policy in the field of international cultural policy, implemented in the second half of the 1990s, ignited the processes through which the Netherlands established itself as an intrinsically international contemporary art platform. Within these government-directed guidelines, art academies were encouraged to have an international orientation, new residency programs for foreign artists were set up, art festivals began working with clearer international profiles, and international networks were encouraged to set up their headquarters in the Netherlands. In the political jargon, the way this change was promoted contained an interesting contradiction because it was an 'international' policy that focused on the Netherlands and its own cultural climate. In other words, it was a policy intending to let the world come to the Netherlands instead of other way around; an amusing parallel to the Dutch practice of reclaiming land from the sea. However crucial this must have been for the revitalisation of the art world at a certain point, such reorientation of international cultural policy seems to have posed precious little active challenge to Dutch art practitioners in the long term, which would have led to strong international positioning. Ultimately, a metaphor of a simulator comes to mind: as a practice that generated test conditions approximating the actual circumstances, produced around a hypothetical understanding of the international reality, and reproducing the co-ordinates of an international arena in a small-scale, model format, in safe proximity to home waters. All this occurred within the borders of the country, and it was consequently not sufficiently acknowledged that foreign-born initiatives have adapted to the Dutch context, and became system-dependent themselves. Could this be the way that such a self-contained system, which treated the local and international simultaneously with the same instruments, actually caused what we now refer to as a delay or, to put it even more strongly, a disconnection from actual global developments in the arts?
Aware that this is nothing but an artificially abstracted, quasi-historical construct put together for the sake of argument, we could perhaps say that the Dutch international

paradox resides in the fact that in the field of arts this country is intrinsically international, yet does not perform well in an international context. In other words, most art and cultural institutions in the Netherlands present international programs, but few are international players. Could we further say that the Dutch are remarkable model makers when it comes to building and exporting international structures, as well as founding international networks, but these have little content-driven presence in the Netherlands, and do not resonate abroad as Dutch initiatives. For that matter, it could be argued that in the Netherlands the critical art discourse is remarkably disconnected from what is at stake internationally, as if in splendid isolation from the global context – both in terms of themes under discussion, and the level of intellectual discourse.

Apropos critical art discourse: it is not necessarily the case that the themes and questions dealt with everywhere else in Europe do not appear on the Dutch agenda. Often, however, they are presented as peculiar national news or belatedly, long after they are considered hot topics abroad. The frame of reference of people dealing with or analysing these kinds of issues in Dutch dailies and art publications is often limited and they display remarkable indifference towards the way colleagues from abroad approach the same subjects. Take the recent preoccupation with 'politically inspired' or 'engaged' art that was treated here as an exclusively Dutch phenomenon! *Vrij Nederland* recently examined the above mentioned 're-introduction of engagement in the field of contemporary art' in an article that refrains from mentioning the many recent publications and symposia on the subject held elsewhere in the world, does not distinguish between 'art activism' and critical political artistic practice, and even succeeds in referring to a non-existent art piece by Santiago Sierra (the performance the author describes is actually a conflation of two other works by the artist)! This is a self-colonising, self-discrediting strategy that cannot be taken seriously and therefore cannot mean anything outside the national context. What weapons could be deployed to fight such ongoing international disqualification?

Before attempting to answer this question, it might be useful to address briefly, one last time, Szeemann's concern about the impossibility of a project called *Visionary Netherlands.* Perhaps we understand all too well that there are more constructive and challenging ways of creating a situation for radical aesthetic and political imagery than the notion of *nation* can provide. It is not necessarily a national spirit that supplies visions. It may be time to demythologise those intangible terms and admit that culture, by any definition, is about people, about remarkably talented artists, writers, and cultural professionals capable of producing distinct ideas and bearing intellectual responsibility for them.

There are numerous talented artists and intellectuals living and working in the Netherlands, who in a fluid way also inhabit an international arena, where they are sometimes cherished more than at home. Without doubt the Netherlands provides a hospitable base in such cases: one can, in the most positive sense of the word, take advantage of both the generous subsidy system and one of the largest, exceptionally well connected international airports in the world, both of which ensure the option of escaping the system for the same reasons that make it worth staying. But hopefully there is a way of creating space for creative people, free of the neutralising powers

of egalitarianism and systematisation, metaphorically speaking, to postpone the
next departure.

Creating real free space for these personalities and individuals ('visionaries') to roam,
create, and develop as they see fit would require profound change, a deliberate decision
to let go, to stop relying on structure. There is no use in creating '*gedoogzones*', areas
where mild law-breaking is accepted, because that would only amount to more of the
same, a kind of tolerance that does not produce content-driven changes. Fundamental
change towards genuine openness is an excruciatingly slow process, a development
that can only occur when we accept the need for 'grey areas' we cannot fully control.
Looking at systems in neighbouring countries, which at first glance seem unregulated
and chaotic, can provide a starting point, but a profound willingness to allow and
encourage the non-defined can only be achieved over a long period of time. Truly
resetting the system, starting from scratch, creating a situation of tabula rasa where
even the most basic notions are rethought would be the only solution. It would be
naïve, however, to hope that such a governmental policy would ever be possible. In the
meantime, awaiting this general deus ex machina awakening, we can and should remain
aware of the following: the arts field must first nourish and challenge itself to create its
own narrative, and it is the responsibility of the policy makers and art administrators to
listen carefully.

We have chosen to speak of imagination rather than facts, to simplify and hyperbolise,
to employ notes, sketches, and questions. We conclude with another anecdote, recalled
by writer Viktor Jerofejev about Stalin. When Stalin's minister of culture complained
to the leader about Soviet writers, Stalin replied, "But I haven't got any others for
you!" No matter how unsavoury the political figure central to this episode, at least
two, if conflicting, conclusions can be drawn for our purpose of searching for the point
where the disenchantment with our Dutch international paradox originates. First,
that something like artistic and cultural production cannot be disciplined or directed
according to the wishes of the politicians or civil servants; and second, if there is a
reason for dissatisfaction about the direction in which the field is developing, it might
very well be an outcome of the very political mechanisms that brought it to life.

Ann Demeester is the director of W139, a production house and exhibition space for contemporary art in
Amsterdam. She is a guest lecturer at the Higher Institute for Fine Arts in Antwerp and the Sandberg
Institute in Amsterdam. Formerly she worked as a journalist and curator.

Maria Hlavajova, curator, has been the artistic director of Bak, base for contemporary art in Utrecht, since
2000. During the Dutch Presidency of the European Union in 2004, she was responsible for the art program
Who if not we should at least try to imagine the future of all this? Seven episodes on (ex)changing Europe.

1 - John Peet, Model makers, A survey of the Netherlands, *The Economist*, May 4 – 10 2002, available online at
www.economist.com/surveys/displaystory

Essay by Ann Demeester and Maria Hlavajova

Reflection? What Reflection?

An American acquaintance of mine wasn't sure which way to look. During a lunch in Amsterdam I'd taken my notebook out of my bag; on the front cover there was a reproduction of an overly-familiar self-portrait by Vincent van Gogh, the paranoid, tormented head that he painted in 1889, a year before his suicide, which currently hangs in the Musée d'Orsay in Paris. My acquaintance asked himself how he was meant to interpret this. A *Dutchman* wandering around *Amsterdam* with a reproduction of a *Van Gogh*: "*How corny is it carrying something like that around here,*" he asked tentatively. He suspected that it was irony, or even a little lame *camp*, on my part, but he wasn't entirely sure. Even in large parts of the United States it would be evidence of a serious lack of a Bourdieu-esque feeling for artistic relationships if you went around proudly with a Van Gogh on your diary; but he didn't know me or Holland well enough to assume blindly that I too had profound ironical intentions with the self-portrait. Maybe it was different in the country of Vincent's birth; maybe here we had an entirely different view of the ubiquitous Van Gogh than on the American East Coast.
I assured him that this was one of the most intense and gripping portraits I knew of – and yet he still looked doubtful. It was as if I'd told him that the Diary of Anne Frank was actually quite moving.
His reaction reminded me of an interview I'd done the year before with John Leighton, the Irish director of the Van Gogh Museum. He described the dilemmas caused by the excessive fame of Van Gogh: there was no difficulty attracting foreign tourists to his museum, every year they came in droves for the unequivocal myth of Van Gogh, publicity was hardly necessary, but it was all the more difficult to get *Dutch people* inside; they considered themselves too familiar with Van Gogh's work to be able to summon any interest in it. Leighton: "There are enough Americans who come here and voice their disappointment that Vincent doesn't look like Kirk Douglas. But it's Dutch people in particular who have the feeling that they know his work through and through. It's become all too familiar."
Try to imagine a similar attitude from the Spaniards, or even the French, towards Picasso. If it's so familiar, what's the work about then? And what does it say to us? This totem of Dutch painting seems to have become the symbol of Dutch indifference – and that tells its own story. At the moment the talk is all about the lack of foreign interest in what's happening in the Dutch art and museum world, but take a look at the one museum where this is absolutely not the problem and you'll spot the same difficulty from a different angle: Dutch lethargy towards its own art.
It's a cruel irony that it's Van Gogh's work that's become so commonplace, as a result of cliché-formation on the one hand and the endless reproducibility of works of art in a mass culture on the other, for if there's one artist who made an effort to breathe new life into a dead reality it's Van Gogh. The same Van Gogh Museum had put on a major exhibition a couple of years earlier devoted to an equally time-worn theme, Van Gogh's failed friendship with Paul Gauguin, and it had shocked me, precisely because the canvases of both painters, one rooted in a French, Catholic, *symbolic* culture, the other permeated with realistic Dutch Protestantism, could be seen alongside each other for the first time, and for the first time I realized the range of their artistic enterprise – and

how much that enterprise still said to our own time, in which the art world has been struck by a sense of acute crisis. These two artists sought each other out because their sublime objectives were apparently the same, to re-introduce the sacred to a tarnished world by means of their transforming gaze, but their visions differed radically, with all the consequences that that entailed. Van Gogh acknowledged the existence of a reality outside his own consciousness. Gauguin acknowledged only the human imagination. How *Dutch* is Van Gogh actually, I asked John Leighton during our interview. "In his obsession with the landscape he's very Dutch. The idea of the landscape as a symbol of the life force, of sowing and reaping, runs like a leitmotif through his work. But his treatment of the theme has nothing Dutch about it. That passion, that intensity he paints with, his vulnerability too, I see all that as un-Dutch. He's so open and direct. He wears his heart on his sleeve. But consider, he spent only half of the ten years he painted in the Netherlands."
Dutch, un-Dutch. The portrait of Van Gogh on the cover of my notebook was, apart from the fact that I still found it surprising in spite of its over-familiarity, naturally also a mild provocation – against the Dutch art snobbery that ensures people no longer cherish their own familiar treasures, and against the eroding effects of our visual culture ("look again!"). But also against Dutch people's general lethargic indifference towards art, even the very greatest.

One of the unexpected effects of globalization is that people do not direct their look outwards, but rather inwards. Seen from a distance it often seems like a re-discovery of the personal, a sudden embracing of a familiar self-image, which exhibits all the characteristics of a nostalgic re-birth – one rediscovers one's language, one's history, one's art, oneself, *precisely* because all these things seem to be threatened by a worldwide forced homogeneity. Such developments seem at odds with the image of a world that is steadily growing more uniform, in which everything and everyone increasingly looks alike; in which the regional, the specifically traditional, is willfully abandoned for the general. You only have to look around you to see that this is not how it works: the people on our planet have never before been in such direct contact with each other, and questions about identity and inalienability have never been pushed so much to the forefront. In retrospect, it's amazing that this reaction was all but unforeseen, as was the fact that the advancing unification of Europe would give rise to a revival of nationalism, for example. It's that pendulum effect – every radical development inevitably leads to a reaction – which in its turn causes a shock, because it doesn't tally with the classical concept of progress in which every ageing world is irreversibly replaced by an entirely new one.
The Netherlands is one of those countries where this unexpected effect has exerted itself most strongly. For a number of years our gaze has been directed firmly inwards, on all fronts – political and cultural. I think this is an understandable reaction to the rather vacant internationalism that gripped the country in the last decades of the twentieth century, that grim tendency to free oneself from everything traditional and what passed for indigenous. Where once people were willfully blind to everything that resembled the anachronistically provincial, that which was seen as cosy, bourgeois, limited, unfree, in short that which could be seen as *Dutch*, now the opposite impulse seems to dominate: people no longer want to see themselves in an international, multilateral perspective. Many of the discussions about the necessity of cherishing one's own culture and history over the last few years have formed a shaky façade

behind which fear and panic lurk, and of course nostalgia, a great deal of nostalgia for what was once thoughtlessly cast aside. The process of individualization that has taken place over the last few decades has produced independent, vocal citizens, but it has also done away with an international vision stemming *from* Dutchness. We are no longer able to see ourselves as a component of a greater whole. Currently, one is a world citizen, a component of an endlessly flexible globalized network of international cultural relations, whether virtual or not, or else one withdraws into a sort of petty Dutchness, which is only concerned with what's right at hand, with what has immediate relevance to the here and now. Either the Netherlands no longer exists, or the rest of the world is dourly ignored.

I think these attitudes are opposite sides of the same coin; the inability to see oneself and one's culture in perspective. Both ways of looking, or rather not looking, testify to a sense of vacancy, an alarming incapacity to look outwards from shared experience. That's what I call Dutch incapacity, and it affects Dutch society on all fronts.

The shrill bickering that has been heard for some time in response to the justly raised question of whether contemporary art is in the midst of a crisis suggests in itself that there is indeed a crisis. But, as has been noted, this crisis has perhaps less to do with the quality of individual works of art than the general conception of the significance that art has for us, or might have. The distressing absence of self-conviction means that the art world cannot defend itself against art-despising populism at home – and therefore can play no significant role across the border either. What are you supposed to answer if essential questions are posed and you only have a handful of fashionable, borrowed words for an answer? Crying out idly that the Netherlands can't possibly have lost its international position in the field of art is pointless if you neglect to entertain the insight that should precede this observation: namely, the answer to the question of why belief in the real social significance of art in the Netherlands is absent, both among the citizens and the representatives of the art world. If we scarcely believe in it ourselves, then how can we convince others? So although it is essential that our look be directed inwards, it should be a critical, inquiring look, which only then can be directed outwards again with conviction.

A painter like Van Gogh was, as John Leighton says, Dutch and un-Dutch at the same time – and that becomes clear as soon as you try to see him in a national and international context. To be Dutch and un-Dutch, and at the same time – this is the task for a Dutch cultural elite that wishes to play a significant role again, both in the Netherlands and abroad. It has to be possible for Dutch culture to rediscover its consciousness without excluding the rest of the world. Ambition is necessary for this, but ambition is useless if it isn't coupled with profound self-investigation. Belief in art precedes a belief in Dutch art.

Bas Heijne is an author and essayist. He has published two novels, two collections of short stories and various collections of essays, among which, *De werkelijkheid* (2004), and his most recent collection, *Hollandse Toestanden (2005)*.

Important International Performances Twice a Month

Johan Simons interviewed by *Bob Witman*

A few weeks ago the State Secretary for Culture said to director Johan Simons: "Where form is concerned, Dutch theatre is fifteen years ahead of its time, don't you think, Mr. Simons?" Simons relied: "I'm sorry, but I don't know how you arrive at that conclusion. What you say is absolutely wrong. It may have been like that during the eighties, but we're living in different times. Content is what's in demand today. You have to dare to pose ethical questions. Theatre has to invite people to think." And people seem to be very suspicious of thinking in the Netherlands.

Director Johan Simons, aged 59, is for the moment the Artistic Director of the ZT Hollandia theatre company, till he moves next season to take over at the NT Gent (National Theatre company of Gent). He has a quarter of a century of theatrical experience behind him in Holland, but he is not optimistic about the future. "We have lost our international connection. I regularly talk to foreign colleagues, people like Gerard Mortier, the manager of the French Opera company. They no longer come to see what's going on in Holland. Nothing ever happens here any more."

And Simons is not in a position to contradict them. "Holland is too scared of being elitist. Theatre directors are terrified of making a statement." Anything difficult is suspect, even thinking. "In Germany, the intelligentsia still goes to the theatre. They are still passionate about thinking. Polemics is alive, just like in France." In Holland, everything has to be accessible to everyone. "The result is that subsidized theatre has shifted heavily towards entertainment: the cruder the better." Simons has nothing against entertainment. "But theatre isn't entertainment for the masses. Nor should it aspire to be so."

From the eighties onwards, Simons became known, with Hollandia, for his theatre-on-location: pieces such as *Stallerhof* (The Stable Yard, 1991, a countryside drama set in an abstraction of a farm), *De Perzen* (The Persians, 1995, a Greek tragedy in a breaker's yard) and *Val van de Goden* (Valley of the Gods, 1999, set in a shipyard in Antwerp). For him, theatre has to be 'political'; it should somehow take the day's pulse. And he finds this lacking in his Dutch colleagues' work just as he finds the Dutch theatre lacking in great thinkers. "I don't see them; no one seems capable of sharp analysis and clear thinking. There isn't anyone like Rem Koolhaas who can pull things up onto the next level." People work hard in the theatre, and there are some wonderful productions. "But they don't show the way forward. It's not controversial and it doesn't provoke discussion."

Countries need their elites: Holland too. "As theatre people we shouldn't be afraid to create productions for a small group. Subsidies are meant for experimentation, for the search. Not for putting bums on seats." This Dutch fear of thinking, the fear of being elitist, has arisen over just the past five years, thinks Simons. "The elite can sharpen our thinking. They can give direction, and contribute to envisaging how society should be. We have to shoulder that responsibility. If you don't want it, you just get little Jan Mulder types: people who say whatever comes into their heads."

Along with Paul Koek, Simons set up Hollandia in 1987. In 2001 the group merged with the Zuidelijk Toneel to become ZT Hollandia. In recent years, Simons has increasingly directed abroad. In particular, the Germans are enthralled by his earthy theatre-on-location, which almost always has contemporary punch. "Don't misunderstand me,

I thank God on my bended knees for what Holland has done for me." But at a certain
point the end comes in view. "Then you stop growing. I can't keep on getting excited
about the same old critics, the same old reviews. The journalists don't explore the
themes in my work. There's no polemical debate in the papers." And Simons admits his
own guilt. "Could I say the Nationaal Toneel company has come to a standstill over the
last few years? No, I couldn't. It wouldn't be fair to my colleagues. But I should say it."
In Belgium and Germany, he does see debate taking place. "Hanging outside the
building of the Kammerspiele and the Stadstheater of Munich is a publicity poster for
a show with a picture of the Pope with an elephant's trunk. Local politicians were up
in arms. Frank Baumbauer, the manager, had to fight to his last breath to be allowed to
keep the poster on display. That keeps you on your toes. In Belgium, the Vlaams Belang,
the extreme right-wing political party that was recently forced to change its name from
the Vlaams Blok when it was banned by the Belgian courts, wrote: 'Stop all subsidies for
municipal theatres in Gent, Brussels and Antwerp'. Because they think the work is too
experimental. Well, you know who your enemy is then. You know you're making theatre
on the razor's edge."
It's so safe in Holland. Perhaps subsidy is a factor in this. There's no incentive
to experiment. "As someone responsible for theatre you are rarely asked critical
questions. I'd like it if a manager or the director of a theatre were to oppose me a bit
more often. When I'm directing in Germany, that's what happens. I often ask myself, for
instance: why are they doing this play in heaven's name? In Holland, the choice is so
gratuitous. Leave those plays to the commercial sector. Subsidized theatre is supposed
to do something else." But no one asks Simons that sort of question.
It's high time theatre subsidies were subjected to review. "A group of thinkers,
outsiders, should investigate the subsidy system. It should be turned on its head.
You need to organize it so that in every major company, a supervisory board, people who
know what they're talking about, keep track and criticize those responsible. Producers
and directors should be encouraged to experiment. And by experimentation,
I don't mean making theatre in someone's living room for thirty people."
The drama schools could do with some critical investigation as well. Only one out of
every seven actors who emerge from them is any good. The numbers should be reduced.
"We should only get the pick of the bunch. The schools should turn down more people.
And they should be allowed to kick you out even in the last year if you're not good
enough." And there's another misunderstanding in Holland; that everything has to be
young. "That ruins everything. Everlasting youth. Appalling! Any middle-aged actor is
suspect. In Germany, you've got directors like Peter Stein, Peter Zadek, monuments of
the theatre in their seventies. Even if they have to be held together with tranquillizers,
they put out one production a year that everyone looks forward to. Directing is
a profession that improves with age."
If there's a way of restoring our international significance, Simons sees it in the
programming of international theatre. At the moment, there's really only the
Holland Festival. "In Antwerp, you've got De Singel theatre, which programmes only
international theatre. We should do something like that in Amsterdam: a theatre which
puts on an important international show twice a month. Yes, good grief, that's an idea!
I should do it! But not me alone, we should all do it together, apply for a subsidy: me,
Ivo van Hove and Theu Boermans."
Holland does not have a theatrical tradition like England, France or Germany. That
used to be an advantage. During the eighties, when Dutch theatre, unencumbered by

history, was able to create new theatrical forms. But that path has reached a dead-end. "I'm going to direct a number of operas for Mortier in Paris. When you walk across the stairway in the old Palais Garnier theatre, you're aware it's the stairway described by Proust. At the barre you see little ballerinas, just as Degas saw and painted them. You really feel the tradition. That doesn't exist in Holland. But a new elite that wants to create a tradition like that: that's the way we need to go."

Bob Witman heads up the art editorial staff of *de Volkskrant*. He has written about cultural politics, architecture and art since 1996.

Malaise – the Opportunity of a Lifetime
Future Prospects for International Cultural Exchange

The current cultural malaise must worry those who closely follow developments in Holland and in Europe in general. But the symptoms of malaise are also interesting, as they present us with countless challenges. And these symptoms are not limited to Holland. Those even remotely interested in the situation in Western European countries will be forced to conclude that the symptoms are the same. They will also draw parallels between the difficulties in the field of culture faced by governments in the various countries, when confronted with a world which is constantly on the move. Western Europe, immersed in unmistakable gloom, needs someone to take a disappointed, even critical look at it.

It is no big secret that most organizations dealing with modern art have seen their budget dwindle sometimes drastically over recent years. At the same time, they have faced new challenges, such as competition from local art organizations, rivalry from far more spectacular forms of culture (the media, film), the redefinition of their role, the internationalization of contemporary art, and art production costs necessitating the use of other methods of financing.

It seems to me that we are at a turning point in the development of our present day history: the end of the welfare state (declared as long ago as the seventies) and a strong increase in international interaction in the politico-cultural field, emerging from the much-discussed globalization (by artists too). Within the context of a globalization which has seen the birth of both local features as well as a multi-polar world – about which we may rejoice – it is inevitable that international cohesion will ultimately undermine local systems. New trends and customs are emerging from this cultural restructuring, and cities, regions or organizations unable to adjust are being wiped off the map. The speed and force with which these phenomena occur are often overwhelming to organizations in the various countries in which other metropolises, beside Paris, New York and Berlin, could play a leading role - if that is still possible? Which direction should international politics take to support artists from our various countries, beside the historical biennials and the rise of a new generation of international events, now too numerous to count? The symptoms are global and the situation in Holland is only one part of this drama, coloured of course by a local scenario with a very specific background.

Look around us

—

In the context of international instability, ruled largely by economic and informational flows, habit may tempt us to withdraw into our own identity, and to look for reassurance in carefully selected chapters from our own history. This would be a daring response to the problem, running counter to the prevailing energies holding the world (or failing to hold it) in balance; even counter to the construct of our own identity in international context, and therefore counter to the evolution of our own culture. The problem cannot be considered or solved solely in its national context. This would not ring true with artists' requirements at present, nor with the reality of the 'space they need to survive'. We need to take current needs into account: nowadays, artists can only function

in a production network which surpasses national borders. Most artists tap into
international trends, cross borders and produce and promote their work in complex
ways. Meeting other cultures, other ways of doing business, and other forms of intellect
is no longer simply a humanistic requirement or a political-intellectual attitude. These
confrontations completely suffuse our image and our experience of the world, in all its
richness and increasing complexity. In these times, when people with different cultures,
religions or ethnic backgrounds are being stripped of their individuality, and especially
when certain clichés and dogged opinions are being repeated more and more often (in
more and more EU countries too), these meetings allow the analysis of present-day
cultural issues (on which much depends) to regain their complex form.
For this, we need to look around us. When Holland occupied the Chair of the EU, our
attention was focused on the realization of several modern art projects. This was
a great opportunity for being confronted with artistic practices in East European
countries featuring intense political, cultural and social phenomena. It seems to me
that this could be to our advantage, both intellectually and methodologically. To give
an example: apart from being confronted with other facts, other ways of thinking
about and formulating our relationship with the world, it would seem to me of great
importance for instance, to analyze the way in which these experiences can contribute
to restating the balance between aesthetic practices and politics ('*le partage du
sensible*' (sharing the perceptible), according to philosopher Jacques Rancière).
The artists taking part in a project such as 'Who if not we should at least try to imagine
the future of all this?, 7 episodes on (ex)changing Europe' have given us a tremendous
stimulus in this sense, which can influence both the way we mount exhibitions and the
nature of present day art itself.
In this kind of meeting with other cultures, we can find the answers to the crisis we
are facing: the way we present art and how we reformulate our thinking about it; the
rediscovery of new practices; breaking with old customs; anticipating future trends;
being inspired by other ways of thinking; giving space to artists, curators and critics
for other rationales; putting up big, imaginative, demanding, ambitious exhibitions;
refusing all forms of laziness; acquiring a good, well-founded, business-like vision on
present-day artistic trends. In this way, a country, region or organization can refocus
international attention upon itself. Instead of conforming to present international
standards, giving innovative responses and being especially receptive to current forms
of present-day art will enable us to reconnect with international culture. Holland has
long enjoyed the reputation of thinking up new practices, and used to exert a strong
attractive force on professionals from all over the world. This was, not unimportantly,
of considerable advantage to artists, designers and architects. It would be a sign of
ambition to take this line of thought as the basis for reflection or policy.

Government as regulating factor

—

It is clear that from now on, it will be difficult, even in countries where government
policy is most generously disposed towards culture, to artificially lay down or create
a global cultural image which goes against the evolution of the time or fashion. But it is
possible for micro-politics to create conditions for international exchange, and *ad hoc*
to think up means for better cultural co-operation, which is essential to artists.
In these times in which government budgets confront considerable deficits, in which
demands from society tend towards division, in which the logic of world economics

has a tendency to rebel against over-involvement with cultural matters (threatening even the expression of cultural diversity), the question is whether there are still other ways of functioning to be found. In a growing number of countries, there is more and more pressure being brought to bear on organizations to find 'new' financing as from sponsoring and private investors. In every country, this pressure is nothing other than the widespread symptom of an arts system being stimulated to rediscover itself, with the danger, sometimes, that it will increasingly resemble the entertainment or cultural event model or that pragmatic economical policy will triumph over artistic creation or reflection.

How, in this sort of context, can government (the State, region, province, organization) present itself as a regulating factor for international cultural trends? It must be clear that the answer to this question depends not only on the government. International cultural politics is only one of the factors in an increasingly complex situation: the private players, the organizations, the artists themselves and the media all carry equal cultural responsibility. The current discussion in France about putting the network of French institutes on the international map, about their functions and privileges, means and effectiveness, demonstrates that beside Holland, there are other countries taking part in this debate.

It would then seem to me that the logic of internationally promoting artists (which would entail their acquiring an international platform for work and discussion) in this case corresponds with the logic dictating the work of every organization for present-day art: the requirement to understand the world's cultural mechanisms and their local transcription, and for openness towards the modernity and nourishment of a certain area, plus the necessity for producing institutional forms and methods suited to artists' needs.

Flexible organizational tools

—

When I raise the idea of micro-politics, this means that international cultural action can be seen within the framework of cohesion between networks and their immediate surroundings, of analysis of the immediate field of activity and of the development of adequate, broadly applicable tools.

These organizational tools do not have to be unwieldy machines. They should, to a high degree, be flexible and adaptable, so they can be adjusted to suit rapid developments in the art world. They should not only be oriented towards territorial thinking (promoting artists, designers and architects from a particular country or particular region or city of a country), but they should also be oriented towards influential international or inter-regional networks. They should be based on an accurate analysis of their range of influence, on precise knowledge of policy guidelines and programmes of the organizations with which they will be working, and on good relationships with the people at the head these organizations. Finally, these tools should take into account a general social phenomenon: the specialization and professionalism of organizational structures.

What concrete forms might these tools take? Small agencies for multilateral co-operation, headed by managers from the exhibition and production worlds? Production platforms specialized in offering advice and expertise to those involved in particular areas of the arts (museum directors, independent institutes, artists, collectors, journalists and critics)? Simple globe-trotters in the arts, who, equipped with computers and mobile telephones, ever-patiently plod away at mending broken connections in the dialogue or at creating the conditions necessary for dialogue? Let us call to mind the historical role played by individuals, whether artists, curators, critics or others, in communicating and sharing aesthetic values and artistic principles. Along with Germany and France, Holland has an excellent infrastructure for modern art, design and architecture. Some artists from a new generation, whom I have met since I came to Holland, manifest an unmistakable energy and inspiration. The malaise apparent in major European cities is in no way a synonym for decline. These times give us a unique opportunity to think, beside the way in which organizations can function, about what is possible in the field of international cultural exchange. It is up to us to rediscover, to dream up ideas, to believe in them and to act.

Thomas Michelon, an art historian, has been cultural attaché of the French embassy in the Netherlands since 2002. He previously worked for art institutions in France and Germany.

Always a Free Port
Alida Nelso interviewed by *Bob Witman*

In her wallet Alida Neslo (Paramaribo, 1954) carries a black-and-white photo of
four young girls in dresses, posing for the camera at a school in Suriname. The
Creole, second from left, is herself. Next to her is the Jewish daughter of a soft drink
manufacturer. To the right is a *buru*, the local word for a white person born in Suriname.
On the far right is a Chinese girl. "When I looked at that photo again, I realised that in
Suriname I had never been conscious of differences in origin. That only began when I
came to Europe."

The whole debate about Dutch culture and identity is a rearguard action, she feels.
"Two hundred years from now Europe will be a melting pot, just like Brazil and Suriname.
By that time it won't matter where you come from, only what you are."
But watch out – because before we reach that point, blood is going to flow.
The Netherlands worries Alida Neslo. Dutch art worries her. "There is so much fear and
so little curiosity." Okay, perhaps it *is* frightening with all these new people. But that's
inevitable. "The idea of keeping the country pure goes deeper than conservatism.
It's a convulsive reaction." Fear itself is a greater danger than all the new influences put
together. "All that crap about our identity, dammit. Haven't we always been a free port?
That's our identity!"

Alida Neslo is an actress, a director and a theatre educator. She studied at the theatre
school in Belgium and joined De Nieuw Amsterdam theatre company in the early
nineties. What struck her then was how different the artistic climate of Amsterdam was
from that of Belgium. "You get a long way in the Dutch art world without ever taking a
good look around you." The subsidy system provides security. "What's missing here is
urgency, art at the cutting edge – like what's being made now in Cuba, or China." Even
Belgium is less lethargic, because subsidies there are not so common. "If you were to
ask me which Dutch groups really catch my curiosity?" After a pregnant silence she
says that Made in da Shade does some interesting things. But that's as far she'll go.
When Alida started working at De Nieuwe Amsterdam, she found the transition to be
greater than when she came from Suriname to Antwerp in the early eighties. "Actors
don't dare to trust their instincts here. In Flanders, acting comes from the gut. "Whether
it's shit or not, let it out. You don't know exactly what's going to happen, but you go on
stage anyway. Here, people sit back in their chairs, read the text, and then read it again.
It took me a while to get used to that way of rehearsing, in which everything is reasoned
out beforehand." In the Netherlands, she says, people want to know how things will turn
out. It makes you wonder whether it's an accident that the word 'apartheid' only exists
in Dutch. That compartmentalised way of thinking. A pluralistic society is not tidy; it's
chaotic, and communications are erratic and full of conflict. But that's not by definition
wrong. In the Netherlands, people are only satisfied when everything is neatly put into
its own place and the steps are scrubbed." Jetty Mathurin has a good joke about this.
"Every culture has its spiritual water to which it ascribes special powers – Florida
water, rosewater. And the Dutch? They have Glassex."

At DasArts, the theatre school she directed from 2000 to 2004, Neslo asked the
students to think about how they should respond to the world. "This has nothing to
do with pamphlets or making political theatre. It has to do with the world in which
you live, for which you bear responsibility. You can't separate art and reality." Her
predecessor at DasArts was Ritsaert ten Cate, who told her that the school engaged
guest lecturers from everywhere. "But they were all Westerners. I brought in guest
lecturers from Asia and Africa." The student exchange program was a one-way street,
too. "Students indeed came to us, but you also have to go abroad and look yourself. You
need that context." This one-way traffic surprised her. There really is no excuse for the
Dutch not to be curious about other cultures. "Although there *is* an excuse the other
way round – if you live in the desert in Timbuktu, I can understand it. But we're rich; we
can't permit ourselves not to be curious. What I'm saying is nothing new; Dutch artists
travelled abroad in the past. You mustn't just sit there and gaze at your navel. I say to
my students, "The Milky Way is in the centre of Amsterdam, but Amsterdam is not in the
centre of the Milky Way."

If you were to make Neslo Secretary of Culture tomorrow, the first thing she'd do
would be to lock horns with the Minister of Education over art education. "The whole
Western educational system has come to a standstill; it's entirely based on the ideals
of the Enlightenment. What a misconception – the Enlightenment purportedly placed
human beings at the centre of existence, but at the same time they were being sold as
merchandise. Liberté, egalité, fraternité – bullshit. The idea of equality is old-fashioned;
what it should be is liberté, diversité, fraternité. It's time for Enlightenment 2!"
There is so much knowledge in this country, she says, but so little wisdom. "And people
have learned precious little from the colonies. If you tell an Englishman that curry
comes from India, he is insulted; he thinks it's English food. And how many Dutch
people know one word of Surinamese? Not many, I think." Because Dutch artists too
often lack the urge to look outwards nowadays, they have no connection with the rest
of the art world, and their art lacks urgency. "You really need to know what's going on
at the biennials of São Paulo and Shanghai."

For Alida Neslo, a European is a person in transit. Everyone is on the move, which
means the question of where you come from is no longer so very important. Younger
people have much less difficulty with this concept than the older generation, she says.
"Young people live from idea to idea, from standard to standard, from ideology to ideology.
You must not be afraid to exchange your standpoint for one that is more adaptable.
But she does see promise in the younger generation, such as Mimoun Oaissa,
the creator of the film *Shouf Shouf Habibi!* "I saw him when he arrived at De Nieuw
Amsterdam. He has so much talent; everybody wanted to do something with him. I said,
'You have to find your own way. You're from two different worlds, you're the future.' Look,
when he shows a bare shoulder in the film, do you know what that means? A Moroccan
boy is naked! That goes much further than a Dutch actor who drops his pants.
We already know about that. When a Dutchman drops his pants, it's not an urgent matter."
Soon she will be going back to Suriname, fulfilling an old promise to herself. Although
if you were to ask her tomorrow to hold Dutch cultural subsidies up to the light, she
would publicly wonder why traditional cultural institutions like the Concertgebouw
Orchestra shouldn't seek alternative financing. "The Dutch business community is so
rich. But you have to go about it cleverly and speak their own language." She would

like to set aside money for what she calls 'eureka groups' – those who are seeking new values in our society. "We used to send people to the other side of the world in flimsy little boats without knowing where they would land. It all comes down to whether you are curious enough, sharp enough." So many groups lean back comfortably on state subsidies without asking themselves what they have to offer society. She quotes an American student who stood up at a conference on multicultural arts and bluntly said, "Oh, Europe – so much history, and no future."

Bob Witman heads up the art editorial staff of *de Volkskrant*. He has written about cultural politics, architecture and art since 1996.

Culture for Real
Masuhiro Sato interviewed by *Ed van Hinte*

The coincidence is striking. Thonik, working on the design of this book about Dutch international cultural politics, temporarily employed the services of a designer from Japan. While Thonik has only once ever had to change a concept, the basic idea behind a design, because it had been done earlier by someone else, that occurred in Tokyo over a year ago, and the designer who beat Thonik at its own game, doing graphic work for a furniture exhibition in his spare time, was Masuhiro Sato. The show featured seventeen designers and design groups, one of which was Droog Design. So when this same person, Masuhiro Sato from Tokyo, applied for an internship at Thonik the studio took him on, as he was obviously an outstanding designer. At the same time they foresaw a difficulty. Mas had nine years of professional experience as an art director at Hakuhodo, a large Japanese advertising agency, which employs about 3000 people and works for large companies like Nissan and Coca Cola, which is far beyond what one would expect from someone doing an internship with simple assignments.

But Mas, short for Masuhiro, wanted to come to Thonik, not so much because he was interested in Dutch culture, but rather because he wanted to learn more about the ideas behind Dutch design. He says: "I already knew about Rietveld and Total Design, but I didn't know they were from the Netherlands. After discovering Droog I began to notice their books. I really loved them and I saw that Thonik designed them. The concepts of these books were clear and their design intrigued me. I was impressed by the way in which Thonik was able to communicate with people, through typography rather than through images. That, I think, is typical for Dutch graphic design in comparison with what is common in other European countries. I would really like to import this typographic style into Japan, though this is not easy because of the differences between alphabet letters and Japanese characters."

So Mas wants to learn how graphic design concepts are developed in the Netherlands, pick up the philosophy behind them and come to grips with the way they are explained to customers. He admires the attitude of the commissioners he has met in the Netherlands: "Dutch clients and government seem to understand the value of creative quality. They support culture and value the beauty of creation. When I return to my company I would definitely like to shift the emphasis in my work from advertising to cultural projects to enrich Japanese people emotionally and creatively. And although my contribution will be modest I hope to be able to make a difference. It will not be easy though, because Japanese companies and government hardly ever spend money on cultural projects and the Japanese don't try to improve their own culture."

Meanwhile Thonik has overcome the difficulty of the involvement of an over-qualified intern by getting him involved in projects. The Municipality of Amsterdam assigned him the task of developing ideas for a poster, parallel to the 'regular' Thonik project, for celebration the 25-year reign of Queen Beatrix. Even though Amsterdam preferred the Dutch design, Thonik's Thomas Widdershoven wouldn't have minded at all if the city council had gone for the Japanese option. Mas was also commissioned to design an

image essay for this book on what strikes him about Dutch culture, thereby engaging him in its concept.
Mas thinks this is funny: "Dutch designers made me think like this."

Ed van Hinte is an industrial designer and teacher of design at ArtEZ in Arnhem. As a freelance publicist and
editor he has written and edited several books on design.

This publication is a joint publication by the Service Centre for International Cultural Activities (SICA), the Mondriaan Foundation, the Fund for Amateur Art and the Performing Arts and the Foundation for the Production and Translation of Dutch Literature.

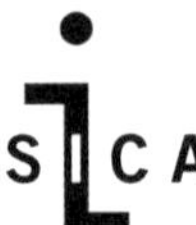
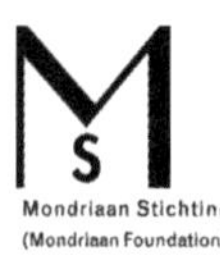
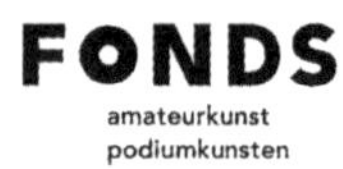
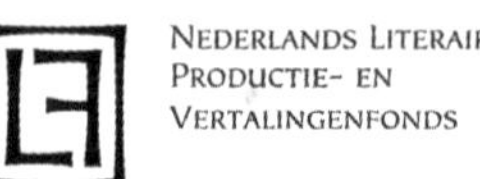

Composition, compilation and editing
—
Ben Hurkmans, George Lawson,
Gitta Luiten, Henk Pröpper, Taco de Neef,
Femke van Woerden-Tausk

Production
—
Taco de Neef
Femke van Woerden-Tausk

Copy editing
—
Rowan Hewison (Pittwater Literary Services)
John de Vos (Redfox)

Translation
—
Jane Bemont, Helen Borkent-Richardson
Paul Evans, Donald Gardner, Michael Gibbs,
Anita Joppe, Dawn Mastin

With thanks to
—
Marieke van Schijndel, Ellen Adriaanssen,
Barbera van Kooij

Design
—
Thonik

Printing and lithography
—
Drukkerij Onkenhout B.V.

Binder
—
Nouveau Delcour Bindtechniek, Hilversum

Distribution
—
NAi Publishers
Mauritsweg 23
NL 3012 JR Rotterdam
The Netherlands
www.naipublishers.nl

Available in North, South and Central America
through D.A.P./Distributed Art Publishers Inc,
155 Sixth Avenue 2nd Floor,
New York, NY 10013-1507,
Tel 212 6271999, Fax 212 6279484,
dap@dapinc.com

Available in the United Kingdom and Ireland
through Art Data,
12 Bell Industrial Estate,
50 Cunnington Street, London W4 5HB,
Tel 208 7471061, Fax 208 7422319,
orders@artdata.co.uk

Printed and bound in the Netherlands
ISBN 90-5662-463-6

© 2005 All rights reserved. No part of this publication may be reproduced, stored in a retrieval system, or transmitted in any form or by any means, electronic, mechanical, photocopying, recording or otherwise, without the prior written permission of the publisher.

This publication has been made possible by financial support of the Fund for Amateur Art and the Performing Arts.